Experiencing God's

Priceless, Precious Promises

Dawn Densmore-Parent

Dedication

My prayer is that the accounts contained within this book will encourage you to commit to be 'sold out' to the message of Jesus Christ with a deep desire to be available to Him 24/7/365 in a walk of yielded obedience, giving praise along the way to His Holy name!

"Surely I come quickly".
"Amen, even so, come, Lord Jesus"
Revelation 22: 20

My Thanks

My deepest gratitude and thanks to those who are included in this book, as well as to those who encouraged and supported me during the process of writing with thoughtful feedback.

My thanks especially to Fabien Parent for his love and care for me and my family! My thanks also to my family members, who daily inspire me and help me to 'want to 'do' and 'be' my very best each day!

Cover Design by: Tamara Smith, UVM Print and Mail, VT

Scriptures are from the Holy Bible, King James Version

©Copyright 2019

978-1-7342353-0-2

INTRODUCTION

For I know the thoughts that I think toward you, saith the Lord, thoughts of peace, and not of evil, to give you an expected end (Jeremiah 29:11).

And ye shall seek me, and find me, when ye shall search for me with all your heart (Jeremiah 29:13).

Serving God has blessings for believers right now, as well as eternal rewards. When we walk in love towards God and one another we create a foundation for the Lord to reveal Himself to us in extraordinary ways.

Contents

Chapter 1 9
Heirs 9

Chapter 2 13
Divine Providence 13

Chapter 3 29
Be Faithful 29

Chapter 4 37
Love One Another 37

Chapter 5 43
Have Courage 43

Chapter 6 49
Gain True Happiness 49

Chapter 7 53
Find Real Love 53

Chapter 8 63
Be Thankful 63

Chapter 9 69
Praise Him! 69

Chapter 10 81
Be Ready Always 81

Chapter 11 87
Blessings 87

Chapter 12 93
Be Devoted 93

Chapter 13 97

God Remembers 97

Chapter 14 101

Have A Heart Vision 101

Chapter 15 107

Be Joyful 107

Chapter 16 111

Believe His Promises 111

Chapter 17 119

Be Sure to Laugh 119

Chapter 18 123

Be of Service 123

Chapter 19 131

Have One Purpose Only 131

Chapter 20 137

Celebrate Each Day 137

Chapter 21 141

Live for God 141

Chapter 22 145

Life is Forever 145

Chapter 23 149

Eternity Never Ends 149

Experiencing God's Priceless Precious Promises

Chapter 1

Heirs

"Children are heirs; hence we are heirs of God

and joint heirs with Christ. "

Romans 8:17

What is the value of a soul? What is the purpose of 'life' itself?

The Bible is clear that humans were created and placed on earth for the purpose of giving glory and honor to their Creator.

When the first humans made a decision to operate as independent beings 'separate' from their Creator, a 'door was opened' for evil to enter our world. The Lord honored that choice, and with free will choice came war, chaos and death. The results of that decision were foreknown by God, who promises to work all things together for good to them that love God, and to implement His Plan of salvation for all who will receive it.

That amazing priceless, precious promise of God has actually been fulfilled by the coming of Jesus Christ as the first risen from the dead, alive forever more. Our Redeemer has paved the way for each of us to have fellowship with God, and with one another. He also promises anyone who comes to Him, eternal life!

God's plan was announced by angels to Mary and Joseph, to shepherds tending their sheep in the fields of Bethlehem, and to wise men who followed the star to the location of his birth,

Bethlehem. Why did God go to so much trouble to come down to this earth in the form of a baby who was placed in an animal shelter because there was no room for them at the Inn? Why would Herod, when the wise men did not return with news of their finding him, choose to kill all babies under two years old in Bethlehem?

Thirty-three years later, one of the two thieves who was crucified with Jesus uttered, "Remember me, when I come into your Kingdom!" Jesus's reply was, "Today thou shalt be with me in paradise!" The other thief mocked Jesus, saying, "If thou art the Christ come down off the cross." Two individuals, two choices, one with faith – one against faith.

Such amazing words from Jesus. Such a priceless gift! Eternal life is available for all: we need only ask, like the believing thief! That thief did not have time to make restitution, do good works, or go to the Temple. Jesus himself had asked in prayer to God three times, "If it be possible, remove this cup from me, nevertheless NOT my will but Thine be done."

It is through Jesus's death and resurrection, that God has accepted His sacrifice as payment for sin. Eternal life is available to me and anyone else who by faith believes and asks and receives this forgiveness and follows Him. It is hard for me to understand this amazing 'exchange' of His death that secures 'eternal life'. In heaven there is no more pain, no more suffering, no more tears, ONLY joy and peace forever and ever. Heaven is perfect, no thorns or weeds, where nothing ever dies. Flowers, birds, animals, and us former human beings, are transformed by His Holy Spirit to a place where God is loved and honored and where people love in word and in truth and in deed.

To be an 'heir' means to 'inherit' all that the Father possesses.

In addition to all of this, God's promise is to reward those who choose to walk the narrow path while on earth, those who believe that Jesus is the way, the truth, and the life. Think beyond living the life of a billionaire; think of life with no need that is not met, that has continual joy, peace and love! All of this is promised to those who love Him, and best of all eternal life lasts for EVER!

"Eye hath not seen, nor ear heard neither have entered into the heart of man, the things which God hath prepared for them that love him" (1 Corinthians 2:9).

These priceless promises of God generate a sense of incredible expectation, awe and wonder.

But most incredible of all, is that these amazing priceless promises can be experienced RIGHT NOW for those who are 'all in', for those who are willing to live their life with the sole purpose of serving the Lord and loving one another. Don't believe it? Read on.

Chapter 2

Divine Providence

Ye have not chosen me, but I have chosen you, and ordained you, that ye should go and bring forth fruit, and that your fruit should remain.

John 15:16

Providence is defined as the protective care of God. We are instructed to:

'Cast all your care upon Him for He cares for you" (1 Peter 5:7).

The Divine Providence Challenge

One Sunday the Pastor's message at church included a question to everyone: "How has the Lord worked in your life?" The Pastor then added a Providence Challenge: "Take time to make a list of the ways in which the Lord has delivered you during your lifetime, and then take time to review that list and then give the Lord your thanks and praise!"

The Providence Challenge I now pass on to you. Right now, stop and write down your own list of what has happened through God's Providence in your own life. You will be as amazed as I was to see how many times the Lord has delivered you, helped you, sent someone to you, and answered your prayers. This life on earth is full of challenges we must face and go through. We are told to expect problems. The apostle Paul dealt with many trials (2 Corinthians 11:26-27).

My life had its own set of 'dangers, toils and snares' that required prayer and the Lord's help to get through. Each Divine Providence circumstance requires the exercise of the same kind of faith Paul used. When I look back, I can see how God has taken each situation which seemed large at the time, and worked all for good in answer to my prayers.

Number 1: Black Sheep

When I was young, my older sisters designated me as the 'black sheep' in the family. I have been told that almost every family with more than one child has one! My family lived on a dairy farm. My claim to fame for this designation, was that I wanted to be dressed totally in 'white' and I also enjoyed playing with dolls. At an early age, I was given an opportunity to exercise courage and walk around a corner of our driveway knowing my sisters would pick on me for being dressed in white and having my doll in my stroller and for playing with her. But I prayed and decided I would 'go around that corner' even though I was afraid to face them, I was willing to fight to keep my doll if I had to! When I got around that corner, no one was there!

Our farm house had three levels. My family lived on the second and third floors and my grandparents lived on the first floor. It was my grandmother who encouraged me, and loved me when my siblings rejected me for being 'different' and not a 'tom boy'. Through her, the Lord provided me with a safe place to go. Without my grandmother my childhood would have been a lot more challenging.

One Christmas when I was young, I was told there would be no presents under the tree for me from any of my family members. That promise was fulfilled. I attempted to avoid the shame it would create by purchasing a piggy bank 'globe', and wrapping it as a gift for me, and placing it under the tree. Unfortunately, I was caught in the act of doing it. When it was taken out from under the tree and handed back to me, I took that present and put it right back under the tree, even though everyone knew it was a gift from 'me' to 'myself'. The sad part was that on Christmas Day, each of them felt bad that they had done what they did, and I was actually okay with it all!

Number 2: Ringworm the Cat

Our farm barn had a lot of cats with the purpose of taking care of mice. One year there were kittens and each of the kittens got claimed by my sisters leaving me without any kitten. But there was one adult male cat called 'Ringworm' who was missing his tail. He was called "Ringworm" because he had ringworms, a circular rash under his fur in different places, that when touched could get on your skin and give you ringworms too! His tail had been cut off by the blade of the motor that drove the milking machine when he had jumped on top of the milking machine motor for warmth. My family members designated "Ringworm" to be my cat. My refusal to accept Ringworm as my cat, did not change their designation. Amazingly, we actually all felt sorry for Ringworm, and had they not designated him as mine, he still would have been cared for!

The amazing irony of it all, is that each of these circumstances helped me at a very young age to understand that hardships draw us to God because they cause us to need God, and when we turn to God, He provides us with His Holy Spirit's very presence.

The priceless gift to me with my stroller and my doll, was once I went around the corner, I heard the Lord audibly tell me, "*Play with your dolls, Dawn, you won't always be able to play with your dolls.*" I played hard that day with my baby doll inside that stroller, up and down the driveway I went again and again! The experience gave me a zeal, knowing it would not always be possible to have that kind of fun! This ONE lesson has helped me throughout my life to take steps of faith that have unknown outcomes, because I know many of my fears will not happen.

The priceless gift for being designated as the 'black sheep' permitted me to have compassion for those who are lonely, hurting and afraid, and my desire to dress in white, made me realize things cannot be 'perfect' all the time.

The priceless gift of Christmas without presents made me aware that the real gift of Christmas is loving God and one another and united me with my sisters in the very pain they too experienced that day! Each of my older family members have apologized individually and collectively many times for their attitude and actions towards me when I was young.

The priceless gift of Ringworm would be that he became my inspiration later in life to ask the Lord for an orange cat just like Ringworm but one that was healthy and that had a tail! I knew the Lord could do anything so I also asked the Lord, for my new orange cat to be female, spade, declawed and free! As unbelievable as it sounds, amazingly the Lord answered my prayer. A man in Rochester Vermont placed an advertisement in the newspaper for his female cat on Christmas Eve! The orange cat's name was "Buffy". When I called at 7 am in the morning, the man told me he would not give Buffy to just anyone, he would have to meet me. A friend of mine drove me 3 hours to meet the man and my miracle cat. Buffy came right to me when I entered his home, something Buffy had never had done before. And Buffy came with cat toys, a litter box, and food. She cried all the way home, but was one of the most loving and beautiful cats I had ever seen! I wept with joy knowing that the Lord had answered my prayer for an orange cat on Christmas Eve in restitution for Ringworm, so many years before.

Number 3: Sexual Molestation

When I was about ten, I was awakened one night with a hand placed over my mouth by our male neighbor who told not to say a word. When I complied, I was sexually molested. I prayed and asked the Lord to help me. I asked God to make it stop. The very next night when the neighbor came to repeat the abuse, my father heard a noise and got up and found him in our kitchen. When he was asked what was he doing, he quickly replied, "I believe I left my wallet on your table and wanted to just come and check to see if it was here, because I cannot find it anywhere, and the last place I had it was here!" I listened as they searched the counters and kitchen and when they did not find it, he left. I thanked and praised the Lord for sparing me and sending my Father into the kitchen to find him! My father, although unaware of it at the time, intervened and stopped this from happening. I was ashamed and afraid to tell anyone what had happened. My solution was to silently make a vow to the Lord that I would NEVER let any man abuse me again. Then, I began to live my life as though 'nothing' had ever happened, and my mind 'blocked' the memory. But the experience which was not dealt with WOULD impact me for the rest of my adult life. The violation would prevent me from feeling safe with any man, and would determine who I married, and would be part of the reason for my choosing to leave my first husband.

Number 4: Unexpected Deliverance

When my friend Patti Pratt died from cancer at 39 years old, her death caused me to go for counseling. Something had broken inside of me and I felt anxious and unable to function. I scheduled a counselling session to discuss 'death'. That session brought me into a room with a man all alone. I did not listen to anything he said to me because of the fear and discomfort of being in the room alone with him. I knew the feelings of fear were not valid. He was there to help me. When I returned home, I told the Lord I wanted to know why I was so fearful. I went and sat on our couch. I told the Lord that I would not get off the couch until I understood why I was so fearful. I sat for a long time and waited. Nothing happened. I got up off my couch and told myself, "This is just ridiculous, it's a waste of time!" As I walked away from the couch, I stopped myself, and made myself go and sit back down. I told the Lord, "I will sit here all night if necessary!" There were magazines on the table in front of me. At one point I picked one up, and then I made myself put it down. "No, I am going to sit and do NOTHING!" This time, as I sat and waited it did not take long for an image to flash in my mind, followed by another and another. I remembered 'visually' the scenes of the molestation that had happened, and that opened the door for my entire life to change.

Number 5: The Encounters

Divine Providence would arrange for me to actually meet and speak to the very man who molested me, and I met him not just once, but twice, and between the two encounters, the Lord provided me with the ability to 'forgive' him for what he had done!

My first encounter with this man happened at a Post Office where I actually spotted him in line ahead of me. I recognized him even 30 years later. I was anxious when I recognized him, but told myself, "He will be through the line and out the door, and you don't have to meet him at all." He did his transaction and headed out the door and I was relieved. But when I finished my mail transaction and turned to go to exit door, I could see him standing next to the exit door. He was just standing there waiting for me, and when I got closer, he went to hold the door open for me. When I reached the door, he greeted me and said, "A gentlemen always opens the door for a lady!" His greeting opened a dialogue of words out of my mouth that I could not stop. I said, "I am a lady, but you are anything but a gentleman!" A line of people gathered, some trying to enter, and some trying to depart as we blocked that entrance area, but I did not move and I did not care. I said, "Do you have any idea who I am? No! No! You do not remember me! But you molested me when I was a child!" The people listened and gasped! He replied, "I am sorry!" I replied, "Sorry does not cut it -you ruined my life!" Those were my last words to him as he exited. I felt quite good about all of it. As I began to leave as well, some of the people said to me, "Good for you!" and "Are you okay?" I replied as I left, 'Yes, I am okay." But as time passed, I felt less good about all of it. I was now just like my sisters had been when I was young, wishing I had handled things better! I actually felt compelled to pray for him. So, I prayed for him and I asked the Lord to help me forgive him, but I told the Lord I did not have any idea if that was even possible.

My second encounter happened years later on a Christmas Eve. I was escorting a couple to lunch as a caregiver. This couple had picked a restaurant and upon entering requested to sit in a booth that was opposite a bar that had a full wall mirror in front of the bar with chairs for people to eat at the bar. As we sat down in the booth, I looked in the mirror and saw a man, and realized it was, again, the man who had molested me. My face must have gone white. After they were seated, and I went to sit down, the couple noticed that something was wrong. The husband asked me, "What is wrong?" I pointed to the man at the bar and said, "That man sitting right there is the man that molested me when I was a child." The husband said, "What are you going to do?" I replied, "Nothing, I have forgiven him!" Both the husband and wife seemed amazed by my statement, and so was I! The waitress came and we ordered. As we sat there, I realized from where I was seated, I could see his face clearly in that mirror, and as I looked at him, I could see that he seemed to be looking at something in the corner of the restaurant. I looked over into the corner of the restaurant to see what was drawing his attention. He was watching a young girl at a table in that corner eating with her family. When she got up to go to the 'buffet table' his eyes followed her. I realized as I watched his head turn, that he was in bondage to the lusts of his flesh! I also realized I was 'free'. There was a true sense of deep gratitude that swept through my heart. When he got up and went to leave, he turned and looked right at me and said, "Have a good day!" I was speechless, but remembered my prayer to the Lord to forgive him and realized I had a small bible book in my purse. So, I quickly found that book and got up to follow him. He was quite a distance now ahead of me, but I shouted, "Wait, I want to talk to you." He turned and looked my way. This time he recognized me. He said in a growl, "What do YOU want?!" The last time we had met was in the Post Office when I had screamed at him. This time, I put my hand on his arm and said, "I want you to know I have forgiven you." He looked very perplexed. I handed him the small Bible book. He said, "What should I do with this?" I said, "I suggest you read it, and I would suggest you say the prayer in it!" Amazingly he replied, "Is that all?" I said, "Yes!" As we parted, I felt a weight lift off my heart. The Lord had arranged on Christmas Eve, the best gift of all for Christmas for me that year! The gift of freedom from 'hate' and that opened a door for me to love again.

Number 6: My Wrong Decision

When I was eighteen, I had a deep desire to understand what 'life' was really all about. That desire caused me to read many spiritual books. One book was titled, 'Three Magic Words' The "Three Magic Words" were: "You are God". I just loved the idea of it! I sat and pondered and accepted the concept and the implications of that statement. My decision to accept this as true, then opened an 'entry' into the spirit world that I could not close. Suddenly an entity attacked me! It felt like a real person, but I could see no one. I cried "Who are you?" The entity simply replied, "You opened the door!" I prayed to the Lord and asked for His help, this was NOT what I expected or wanted! I was being squashed and bursts of electricity were being zapped through my body. Suddenly I saw a 'cross' in front of me and heard a voice say, "Cling to the cross!" So, I did cling to an imaginary cross in my mind. That ended the attack. But it would be this very attack, that would lead me to read the Bible. For the first time in my life, the Bible provided the answers that I had been looking for – words of truth, love and light. The Lord would use that attack to get me interested in attending a Bible Study group. In that group, I would pray with Joyce Carruth a prayer asking God to forgive me and for Jesus Christ to come into my life.

The door I had opened would leave me with a pain in my right back shoulder blade area. To this day, this 'sharp knife pain' still occurs. It seems to be more intense when spiritual growth is happening. The times when I do NOT want to be obedient to God, but in spite of that, make a correct decision to 'push through'. It seems that the enemy uses that as an attempt to convince me to NOT push through but rather to 'change my mind' back.

The Lord has promised to work all for good, and the good that comes from this, is that I actually can get excited about the pain. Whenever I feel it, I know that there is a blessing from the Lord headed my way! For believers who obey, there IS a direct connection between trials and blessings. Within the spiritual world is a balance scale. Our spiritual growth is tested through trials. Like the man called "Job" in the bible who was tried, we are blessed by the Lord for facing and going through trials, and we are blessed when we overcome. Through prayer and faith, we become overcomers!

Number 7: The Accident

One of my skills is an ability to train dogs to heel. When my first husband and I moved to a new town, we had a neighbor who had gotten a puppy golden retriever. I had volunteered to walk and train their dog. One night after work, I rode my bike up the hill to their home and walked their dog. When I got back onto my bike to ride down the hill to my home, the dog suddenly decided to follow me. He ran down the road after me and my bike. I braked to stop, and suddenly the dog was ahead of me and the bike and crossed in front of my bike tire. I turned the wheel of the bike quickly to the right to prevent my bike wheel from running over the dog. The quickness of my turn caused me and the bike to be catapulted through the air - the back of the bike was going over the front of the bike. I clung to the bike handle bars thinking I could pull the bike back up, but I could not. I hit the dirt road hard, and heard 'cracking' and then I was in horrible pain. The owner of the dog ran to assist and helped me to get up. The owner then assisted me with walking home. Once home, my husband took me to the hospital where they gave me pain medicine but that was all they could do. I had a broken collar bone, 3 broken ribs in the front and 2 broken ribs in the back, and a punctured lung. The meds helped but could not cover the pain. I would be out of work for over a month, and it would be a year before I would heal from the injuries. There were days when I was in so much pain that the only place, I was comfortable was in a bathtub full of water. I could not get into the bathtub or out of the tub by myself. My husband also had to help me to sit down and to get up from our couch. I could not lift my body up by myself. One day I decided to just 'feel' as much pain as I could, rather than 'run' away from the pain. I did this to console myself. My consolation was that I knew my body would recover and that in time I would heal and the pain would go away. Experiencing that level of pain made we wonder how people who are in constant pain were able to bear up under the load. My living through this injury gave me compassion for those in pain that I would be assigned to help and care for many years later.

Number 8: A Home & Working 24/7/365

My divorce was a joint decision and it would allow my then husband to be a caregiver for his parents in their home, and opened a door for me to care for my Father in my home. We remain friends to this day. He was happy to learn that Fabien and I had married after we both had been single for many years.

It was my Dad who suggested I purchase a home with a lower level that had an entrance without stairs that we would share. He told me to look at a house his friend's brother owned as an example of something that would allow me to live upstairs and for him to live downstairs. When I looked, they were not ready to sell, and their asking price was more than what I was approved for by the bank. But I became determined to purchase the home if it ever did come up for sale. This began my commitment to work additional jobs. Eventually the home did come up for sale, and I was able to purchase it. Then I continued working additional jobs simultaneously to earn money to prepare the lower level for my Dad to join me. I became a live-caregiver for older individuals enabling them to remain in their homes. My life for seven years was work 7 days a week, 23 hours a day, 365 days of the year with one night off a week. The additional jobs provided funds to subdivide the property, and hire a contractor to build a rental home.

With each assignment, I would ask the Lord to give me an opening to give the people I cared for assurance of eternal life! The Lord was faithful to answer every one of those prayers. I have many people who are on the other side in heaven that I will get to see again in eternity!

I even used my vacation time to work as a substitute legal assistant in law firms which provided me with much needed legal understanding of how to handle renters and rental property.

My father came to live with me in 2008 and remained with me until he went to be with the Lord on December 1, 2015. Fabien and I were married on his farm in 2015. Fabien sold his farm to one of his sons and came to help with my Dad's care. My sister Audrey then came to live with my Dad when he began to need some additional help. An additional bedroom was added to the lower level for her. My sister Treya, moved to VT to be here as well to help with his care, and she purchased the rental home. Now almost my entire family enjoys the two homes that my Father helped to make possible!

Number 9: Lyme Disease

My physical health became a challenge when I was bit by a tick in 2010 and contracted Lyme Disease. Fabien also was bitten by a tick a month later. We both contracted Lyme Disease. We both were challenged to get out of bed and to even move, and we both were in constant pain. At times it seemed like our lives would never be without pain. It would take several years of daily treatments for us to feel better. We are both now Lyme Disease survivors. We keep Tick Spray on when we are outside, and now warn others to be aware of the danger of getting bitten by ticks. The International Lyme Disease Association (ILAIDS) holds conferences each year around the world. Their bottom line is that Lyme Disease can be treated and there can be years of dormancy followed by flare ups. Even now, mold, toxic chemicals, or household cleaning products, can cause flare ups that require supplements to feel good again. But having Lyme Disease has made me appreciate the simple things of life, and made me grateful for every day!

View your own Divine Providence list with 'spiritual eyes' and you will see that the Lord has been with you, too, for it is 'in Him that we live, and move and have our being" (Acts 17:28).

Look Ever to Jesus - He'll Carry You Through - Horatio R. Palmer 1868

Yield not to temptation, for yielding is sin;
Each victory will help you some other to win;
Fight manfully onward, dark passions subdue;
Look ever to Jesus, He'll carry you through.

Ask the Savior to help you, Comfort, strengthen, and keep you;
He is willing to aid you, He will carry you through.

Shun evil companions, bad language disdain,
God's name hold in reverence, nor take it in vain;
Be thoughtful and earnest, kindhearted and true;
Look ever to Jesus, He'll carry you through.

To him that overcometh, God giveth a crown,
Through faith we will conquer, though often cast down;
He who is our Savior, our strength will renew;
Look ever to Jesus, He'll carry you through.

   END

Chapter 3

Be Faithful

Faithful is he that has called you, who also will do it.

1 Thessalonians 5:24

One of the most challenging things for us as believers to do is to share our testimony with others. Yet that is exactly what we are called to do! The great commission is for us to "Go!" Jesus said unto them, "Go ye into all the world and preach the gospel to every creature" (Mark 16:15). Yes, we all have different talents and abilities, but every believer is asked to share their testimony.

My commitment to Jesus was made at age 23, as a direct result of being attacked by demons. Jesus's ability to deliver me from demons caused me to tell Him right out loud, "I know that I am not much, but I am here, send me!" It has taken me many 'uncomfortable fumbled interactions' to become comfortable sharing my faith with others. It is knowing that the Lord is with me that helps me to recover from these learning experiences. We are to be the Lord's hands, feet, eyes, ears, and mouth.

Early in my walk with the Lord, I was drawn to share Bible 'tracts' and Christian poems. This is actually quite amazing, because at 18 when I was reading all those spiritual books, someone gave me a tract. When I read it and saw the word "Jesus" in it, I threw the tract in the trash, and exclaimed outloud, "Jesus has nothing to do with anything!" I find it really ironic that the Lord would compel me now to be the one that gives the small bible books, tracts and Christian poems to others! I created a fabric 'tract pack' for the poems and tracts, so I could carry them easily with me. I take time to read every bible book, every tract and every poem to enable me to know which one to pick for any given situation. And once again ironically when the Lord's Holy Spirit prompts me to share hope with someone, what is given to them, blesses me as well and I thank them for their time, and for blessing ME!

Each day begins with my thanks and praise to the Lord that HE IS LORD! Almost every day I awake with a song in my head, and when I hear it, I often just sing it out loud. Today's song is:

Holiness, holiness Is what I long for Holiness is what I need
Faithfulness, faithfulness Is what I long for Faithfulness is what I need So take my heart and form it, Take my mind transform it
Take my will conform it To Yours, to Yours, oh Lord!

Scott Underwood "Take My Life"

My commitment is to meet with the Lord every day. I want to read the Bible. I want time to write in my journal the verses that jump out at me, and what the Lord shows me from His Word. Daily I write down and tell the Lord about what I need and ask Him for his help for my day. I pray about everything that is on my mind, because I don't want to worry about anything, and this helps me to focus and listen for His still small voice which I can easily miss! Then, I thank him for hearing my prayers, and praise Him for being God and being in control even when things seem so out of control! If it were possible, some days I would stay with the Lord longer, but I have commitments each day that need to be done. So, I ask Him to come along and keep me company. Today is such a day. I had a scheduled appointment to have winter tires put on my car for a very early appointment of 7:30 am. That required my leaving my home by 7 am. My vehicle has a musical CD always in the player for me to turn on or leave off, depending on whether I need to be quiet to process my thoughts, or if I need to pray. When I can, I listen to Christian songs and offer God thanks and praise! This day on my way to the Dealership, I prayed that the Lord would open hearts and doors for me to share my mini bible books and small mini animals. I asked Him to give me the words to say and to help me to listen as well.

Once I arrived the attendant asked for my name, and handed me a form that I signed for work on my vehicle. I said, "We have met before, haven't we? I believe I have shared with you one of my special mini-animals!" He replied, "Yes, you did! You gave me a mini eagle and small book! I still have them!" I replied, "I cannot remember your name!" He replied with his name. I said, "Yes, I remember you now. Thank you for being here this early to help me today!" We both agreed it was hard to get up in the morning. I asked, "Where is your co-worker that usually is here?" He replied, "He has left!" We talked a bit more and I found out where that person went because I wanted to bring him a card and thank him later! He told me and I handed him an invitation to come to the church I attend. I said, "I think you would really enjoy the Bible messages. I truly hope you will come. The service is at 11 am on Sunday!" He replied, "I will certainly consider coming!"

Then I was off to the waiting area. Another customer finished up at another kiosk, and he was right behind me, and we both entered the waiting area. I asked, "Did you lose power during yesterday's storm?" He replied, 'No, I did not!" I continued to share with him the slight damage that we had where I lived, and we both found places to sit to wait for our vehicles. I left the waiting area and went to their coffee station. When I got there, there was another attendant making coffee. I said, "Thank you for making this place so inviting, I really appreciate all that you do!" He smiled and replied, "You are very welcome!" I said, "I have a mini bear to share with you today for 'bearing my burden'. He smiled as he took it, and said, "You have given me one of these before!" I replied, "Well I have a different promise book to go with the bear, as I handed him the small booklet. I said, "We were blessed to not have a lot of damage from the storm!" He replied, "Yes we did not have much damage either." He then left and I went back to the waiting area.

The first man I had met was still the only one in the waiting area, and I called out to him and said, "Good that they have coffee here!" He lifted his head from his phone to acknowledge my comment but did not speak. I prayed that I could be quiet, and the Lord would touch his heart and give me another opportunity to talk with him. I read my book and waited.

Other customers arrived and settled into different spots. One woman came and sat close by me. I stopped reading and said, "You too, up early! I was just told that this is actually the best time to come when all the bays are open and no one is ahead of us in line!" She smiled. I said, "I want to make your day different today!" Then I got up and went and sat next to her and handed her a small sheep. She looked at it as I handed her the small book and wrote the meaning of the S.H.E.E.P. (Spiritual Hope Energizes Every Problem) inside the book. I handed her a poem "Don't Carry the Burdens of Tomorrow" and said, "We all need to remember that we are not alone, that the Lord is present to help and guide us!" She asked, "What church do you belong to?" I responded, "Well, I actually go to several different churches, but mostly to "Northside Baptist Church". I then went back to my seat and read.

An attendant then came for the first man I had met in the waiting room and called him out to the entrance area. I got up and followed him out because I felt God wanted me to talk to him. I went and stood a distance away. The attendant explained that they could not put tires on his vehicle because the rim of the tire was damaged and had a very sharp edge that could cause the new tire to be flat. The man acknowledged that he had hit a curb. The attendant explained that he would have to reschedule to get a new rim and that he could return to the waiting room and they would bring his vehicle out of the work bay so he could come back later. As he headed back into the lobby area, I stopped and said, "I have something for you today." He looked as I handed him a small eagle. I said, "I am not trying to be obnoxious here. Did you know the eagle is the only bird that flies above the clouds, and that is what we need to do in our lives; we need to get up above the troubles, through the Lord's promises that are inside this little book." He took the eagle and the book and I left him and went back to the waiting area. I sent up a prayer for him. I said,

"Lord it is so unfortunate that this man cannot get his tires on today, this is a service center, you would think they could help him and fix the problem for him – just help him for your name's sake and bless him for being open to me!" I went to my table and sat back down to read.

The man came back into the waiting area as well. And more people came and joined us. I continued to ask the Lord for opportunities to give my mini animals, and mini books.

When a client was then called to the front desk and passed my table, I got up and said, "I want to encourage you today with this mini animal, and promise book." She took it and said, "Thank you!" As I returned to my table, I had to go past another customer who had now entered and I spontaneously handed her an animal and promise book as well. She was wearing a black T-Shirt so I gave her a 'black bear' and said, "This is to encourage you to continue to love those around you, we are our brother's keeper!" She smiled, and said "Thank you!"

Finally, my attendant came for me. I got up to leave putting things back into my purse, and pulled out my leather holder to make payment. Just then another woman entered and I went with my purse to share an animal and book with her on my way out. She also was thrilled and said, "Thank you!" As I went to leave, the first woman I had given a Sheep to said to me, "I think you forgot something on the table!" I turned and saw my leather folder on that table. I went back and picked it up and went over to her and said, "Thank you so very much!" She replied, "What was it you left?" I replied, "It is my leather folder with my credit cards in it!"

I reached down and hugged her. Then I walked to exit the waiting room and exclaimed to all that were seated, "I am so heavenly minded, I am truly no earthly good." I heard laughter as I excited the door, and I thought to myself. "Thank you! Lord, for today, and bless all of those individuals who were so patient with me!"

The attendant checked me out and as I paid him, I said, "Thank you for all you do here, especially for helping the man with the damaged rim, it is really unfortunate that he has to come back!" The attendant said, "Oh, his tires are being put on right now! As I was re-scheduling him it occurred to me to check with another person today, and he was able to fix the rim right on the spot, right away!" Quietly I thanked the Lord for answering my prayer for that man! As I left, I said, "I hope I get to see you on Sunday at church!" The attendant replied, "You know, I am actually going to try to make it!"

When I got back to my vehicle, I sat and praised the Lord for helping me to share His promises with every person who had come into that waiting room while I was there, as well as every attendant that I had met. I exclaimed out loud, "Lord only you can open hearts and minds like that! Hear my prayer Lord, and touch each of their hearts and let not your word return void to you!" The verses I had written down that very morning from my time with the Lord were:

Be not afraid but speak and hold not thy peace for I am with thee and no man shall set on thee to hurt thee for I have much people in this city. Acts 18: 9, 10

I will help thee saith the Lord. Isaiah 41:14

For as the rain cometh down, and the snow from heaven, and returneth not thither, but watereth the earth, and maketh it bring forth and bud, that it may give seed to the sower, and bread to the eater, so shall my word be that goeth forth out of my mouth,: it shall accomplish that which I please, and it shall prosper in the thing whereto I sent it.

Isaiah 55:10-11

My hymn lyrics were: "Each victory will help you another to win! Look ever to Jesus he'll carry you through" and "Lord, I commend my soul to thee!"

Truly the Lord hears our prayers and it is not His will that any perish.

Chapter 4

Love One Another

Beloved, let us love one another, for love is of God; and everyone that loveth is born of God, and is of God. He that loveth not, knoweth not God, for God is Love.

1 John 4:7-8

The power and impact of God's love is not limited. The command of the Lord is for us to walk in love one toward another. When we implement this command in our life, we will find ourselves being stretched as we attempt to do things, we think we cannot do.

Love is an Action Word

One of my close friends Suebee called me one day and told me she would need to have gallbladder surgery. She was in a lot of pain, and a surgery date had been scheduled for an operation. The day of the operation, she called and told me, "They are not going to do the operation. It is not my gallbladder; I am full of cancer!" I listened with great sadness. She said, "They want me to do treatments, but I am not going to do treatments." She was told without the treatments she would not last more than a few months. She said, "I was not quite ready to retire, but I am going to retire." We agreed that I would call between 8 and 8:30 am to pray with her daily and we began to do just that. Suebee had an incredible voice, and one day she sang the song to me:

"I have decided to follow Jesus, I have decided to follow Jesus, I have decided to follow Jesus – no turning back – no turning back. Though no one join me, still I will follow; thou no one join me, still I will follow, thou

no one join me, still I will follow – No turning back – No turning back."

Tears ran down my eyes as she sang the song to me. I said, "That is MY song!"

She replied, "I am committed to help my sister with her son's children that she has adopted, but I will not be around to help!" As we talked, I committed to her that I would help her sister with those children.

That week, I arranged to stop to visit her and bring her some music CDs to listen too, and a book to read. My husband, Fabien and I travelled to her home to visit her and drop them off. She looked amazingly well and was able to get around. We hugged and I was able to tell her how much I loved her. So had other visitors that day, so we did not stay long.

When we got back into Fabien's truck to go home, I turned to Fabien and said. "The Lord has impressed upon me that we will not see her again alive." He replied, "She didn't look that bad!" But what the Lord had revealed to me was true, Suebee died within a week.

During her memorial service, Fabien and I met all of her family including her sister and husband that had adopted their son's children. My commitment to help this family would be kept. I arranged to start picking up the children to take them to Sunday School each Sunday.

The whole family has rallied to help one another through the challenge of caring for these children.

A Trial and Unexpected Blessing

As often is the case, challenges do not come alone. Another significant challenge occurred one summer when Suebee's sister's husband had a serious life-threatening issue and ended up in the hospital requiring an operation. Much prayer was made for him and it was with great joy that we learned he would be able to go home. Once he was home, he was unable to do much as he worked to heal from his operation. Fabien and I agreed to mow their lawn and do the trimming that summer and we looked forward to our weekly lawnmowing trip. Fabien is most generous with his time and talents. My trimming was always done before he could finish mowing, and that gave me more time to visit with SueBee's sister!

At the end of the summer, on our last trip to mow their lawn that summer, Fabien noticed when we arrived, that there were piles of 'fill' that had been dropped off to be used to level off a road going into the woods. He told me, "There are pavers on the top of those piles that are 'good' and should not be used that way." He mowed and I trimmed, and when we were finished, he mentioned the pavers again as we got ready to leave. I told him, "We can ask about them for sure." We did ask, and were told that we could have them. We made trips to bring them to our home. Fabien was able to create a 'patio' area with them and set up a 'fire pit' in the middle of them, and we now use this area to gather with our family whenever we can and to visit and enjoy one another.

My Sundays continue to include picking up the children and taking them to Sunday School at Northside Baptist Church, and visiting with the family. The opportunities to be of service continue to evolve. The boys received train sets recently for Christmas and Fabien was able to make tunnels for the trains. One boy had broken a drawer in a bureau, and Fabien was able to repair the drawer and the bureau to hold the drawer.

And it is with great joy that I know that I will see Suebee again in heaven. There we will rejoice together forever at how the Lord took what was 'bad' and created something 'good' from it.

The Coasting Adventure

One fall I travelled to a Woman's Retreat with another close friend Sue. We rode together in a church van driven by Gloria Scribner. The trip down on the van and back provided an opportunity to connect with Sue and others as we got to share our Christian experiences, as well as areas where we needed help and prayer.

On our trip back home as we climbed a very steep hill section on I-89 in lower Vermont, the church van began to sputter and slow down. As we reached the top of the hill, the van came to a complete stop. We were totally out of gas. Gloria was able to pull the van over to the side of the interstate and it was there that all of us sat and discussed what we should do. There were no cell phones back then. All of us began to pray together to ask the Lord to help us! When we finished praying, I got out of my seat, and went to talk with Gloria up front. I had been seated in the rear of the van, and as I walked through the van, we all noticed that the van had started to move forward. Gloria had left the van in gear, and had not shut off the engine. Everyone else then got out of their seats and came forward as well. Suddenly the van began to move a little faster. I told Gloria to put the flashers on and get the van back onto the road and she did. We had been totally stopped at the top of that hill but were close enough to a very slight 'grade' downward. As our weight began to inch the van forward, we knew that the road in front of us was all downhill, and that downhill section was very long and had an exit at the bottom with a gas station right after that exit on the right. Soon we were travelling at the speed of the other vehicles, and no one could possibly know we were out of gas! We encourage Gloria to NOT step on the brakes, just keep going. It was very frightening for all of us, but we knew that if we could keep the van moving, and could get past the stop sign at the bottom of the exit ramp, we might be able to coast right into a nearby gas station.

Gloria was concerned that she would need to stop at the Exit stop sign, but we encouraged her to try not to stop if at all possible. We reached that exit and continued to coast to the stop sign. Miraculously there was no traffic to the left so she was able to coast right through the stop sign and right into that gas station and very close to a pump. We all were very excited; we had made it to the gas station! But were we close enough to the hose?

I got out of the van to see if the hose could reach the tank. Amazingly the hose just barely reached the tank. I am not kidding! I was so blown away, that I got down on my knees right at that gas station and praised the Lord with my hands in the air! Then I got up and pumped the gas!

Gloria Scribner is now with the Lord, but my friend Sue and I continue to be amazed how the Lord was able to give us a coasting adventure in answer to our prayers.

The Fire Paradox

We had a pellet stove installed in our home that has a glass front that allows us to view the flames when the pellets are burning. It is a wonderful sight to see and the warmth of the stove makes our home very inviting on cold winter days in Vermont.

One day as I was washing dishes in the sink in my kitchen, as I looked out the window above my sink, and could see a flame of fire on the lawn in the back yard. My mind was confused to see such a sight. As I looked closer, I realized that the light of the flame inside our pellet stove was being reflected from that stove's glass front door into the kitchen window and then out into our back yard.

I immediately saw a paradox of how the Lord assists us in loving one another. When the Lord asks us to 'Love One Another' that is exactly what he expects us to do. We are to take the 'light of God's love' that he gives to us and project that love to those that we meet just as the light from the flame from the fire was able to be reflected through the glass window to a different place. We can be like that 'glass window' and transfer the light of God's love to others.

And the warmth of God's Love is always with us even when we are dealing with life's trials, like being there to help others, or on a bus that is out of gas, just as the light inside our pellet stove was visible on our lawn outside!

Chapter 5

Have Courage

Be strong and of good courage; be not afraid, neither be thou dismayed, for the Lord thy God is with thee, withersoever thou goest.

Joshua 1:9

Courage requires faith. And trials are the proving ground of faith. The most challenging part of living life on earth is its unpredictability. Bad things can and do happen. Believers are told to expect tribulations, but to be of good cheer because Jesus has overcome the world! The question is whether we are able to go to the Lord in prayer and trust Him with our eternal soul, and still praise him in the midst of a trial.

The Accident

One of the greatest challenges in my life is to 'slow down'. Much of my life has been so full of things that need to be done that I find it a challenge to balance the activities of the day. The desire of my heart is to be obedient to the leading of the Lord, and I have trained myself to instantly respond and this very 'strength' can be worked against me by the enemy if I do not stop and pray.

My Saturdays are busy and this particular Saturday was no different. During a visit with my sisters, I realized that the Post Office would close early that day. My oldest sister said, "Go now!" So, I got up immediately and put on my coat and headed out the door. I got into my car and travelled up the hill to go get the mail. As I looked one way and then the other, I could see that our first snow of the season had covered the ground with white snow. When I looked to the right, I saw a truck a distance way, and to the left, no traffic, so I headed forward to cross the main highway. Then suddenly I hit something – it was a white SUV – right in front of me. The impact was small, air bags did not deploy. But my car bumper was now off in the middle of the road. I backed my car back out of the road back into the street I had just left. My routine trip was now an accident. The white vehicle that I hit was an SUV and damage was done to the back fender above the back wheel. The driver turned the vehicle onto the street and parked around the corner.

I was totally shaken. As I tried to get out of my car, I could not because I was still buckled in. I began shaking so hard that I could not undo my seat belt. A game warden who was at our local store, came to my window to check to see if I was okay and called the Police. I managed to get free of my seatbelt, and get out of my car. I went to check on the man in the vehicle that I hit. He was now out of that vehicle and walking fast behind the car away from me. When I stopped him to talk to him, he said, "You have ruined my life, I am going to jail today! I did nothing wrong! Why did you hit me! I was taking my girlfriend's car to go get her child, and I was driving without a license." I replied, "I am truly sorry! I did not see you at all!" I was stunned, and walked away. I had nothing to say to him.

The Arrest

I went back to my car to wait for the State Police to arrive, and my brother-in- law arrived. He had gone too for a package at the Post Office and had realized it was me involved with the accident. He came and comforted me. Then my sister Treya arrived and did the same. Then my husband Fabien arrived, and said, "Things could have been much worse." He was correct but at the time, I did not feel very happy about any of what had occurred. I had hit a car. How could I have done that!? The State Police arrived and talked first with the man I hit. I watched as the police handcuffed him and put inside the cruiser. Both vehicles actually could be driven and the State Police gave me permission to drive my vehicle to an auto repair shop 3 miles away. The other car would be towed even though the damage to that vehicle was minor, because the driver had been arrested.

The News Article

Two days later, my husband Fabien handed me our local paper. There was a picture of the man I hit, and an article, about my incomplete stop that caused me to hit his car, that caused him to be arrested due to outstanding warrants for his arrest. It was hard for me then, and now to get my head around all of it. Both vehicles could be repaired, and the experience would make me a better driver, as well as everyone in my family, and hopefully has prevented us from other 'accidents'.

The Paradox

The entire Town where I live, is very aware of who I am as well as how much I love the Lord. I hand out gospel poems and stop to talk to complete strangers wherever I go to share the fact that the Lord loves them and is there for them. The last thing I would want to do is cause anyone pain, but here was a situation where a man with a warrant that needed to be dealt with, was apprehended because of my inability to see his vehicle, and my lack of coming to a complete stop, thinking the way was clear to go. Here my name was in the local paper as the 'reason' that the man was arrested. The man is no less loved than I am. I have made mistakes just as he has made mistakes. The forgiveness of the Lord is available to all of us. It is impossible to live life without making decisions that you regret, and that can cause us and others pain and suffering.

The entire experience has changed his life, and has changed mine. He was given the opportunity to clean things up, and I have been given the very same opportunity to remember to stop and pray, no matter how busy the day. The Lord will provide the time I need to do the things that He is asking me to do. This takes COURAGE from moment to moment, to walk yielded to God: not ahead, and not behind but with the Lord's Holy Spirit. To stop and wait, to walk and not run, to stay and not go. This actually requires the exercise of COURAGE!

The Birth of Courage

We stay connected to the Lord by reading his Word daily. When we add to that active prayer time, we are able to 'be in the world, but not OF the world." Doing both together will help us to live our life as 'unto the Lord' and will help us to make good decisions. We have a choice: "Listen to the world's chatter, or choose to listen to His still small voice. I actually work to avoid watching television. For me it is like a huge manure spreader, tossing words and images that spread either fear or awe! Most of the images are like seeds in our minds that draw us away from God. We must be willing to acknowledge our needs to the Lord, and ask Him for His help, as well as for His forgiveness when we feel any separation at all from His presence. Every day provides a variety of snares laid out for us by the enemy that must be identified and avoided for us to stay on track. We must be willing to do whatever is necessary, to work hard, to tell the truth, and to do the very best we can because life itself is 'holy ground'. We must be willing to put on the whole armor of God with the helmet of salvation to be able to overcome patterns of behavior that do not serve us well. When we fill ourselves with God's word, and focus on what is right, and act accordingly, God is well pleased! We would not be impressed by a wedding dress that was amazing but had a black spot on it, or by a restaurant that presented us with a plate that had dried food on it. Therefore, let us work to become unspotted by this world!

The Reward of Encouragement

Fabien's friend who had not been feeling well, invited Fabien to come to his home and hunt with him again. They had hunted together the year before, and Fabien wanted to encourage his friend, so off Fabien went. When he arrived, his friend was not up to going, but told Fabien to hunt without him. Fabien hesitated, but decided he would go and sit in the hunting shack. He no sooner entered and opened the back window, that a deer appeared over the bank. Instinctively, he raised his rifle and shot. He could see he had hit the deer, but the deer had taken off running. Fabien then was compelled to track the deer. It was late in the afternoon, and soon Fabien realized he had to stop tracking. He was unfamiliar with his friend's woods. When he got to his friend's house, they both agreed it was too dark to go back into the woods. Fabien came home and called one of his sons for help in the morning to locate the deer and drag it out of the woods. Fabien had not expected to even see a deer, but now it would be wrong not to go and find it. When they arrived the next morning a coating of snow had fallen making it more of a challenge to track. They followed the path Fabien had taken the night before, and came to a ridge. Each agreed to go the opposite way along that ridge to see what they could find. They both had not walked very far when Fabien saw his son, raise his rifle and put it down, but quickly raise it again and take a shot. His son shouted, 'I just got a deer!" As they tracked Chad's deer, they found Fabien's deer which was covered in snow and would have been very hard to find! How wonderful are the ways in which the Lord works!

When I arrived home, Fabien was processing a deer and I exclaimed, "You found your deer!" He replied, "No this is not my deer!" I replied, "What are you talking about?!' He pointed to the back of or garage area and said, "That is my deer." I looked and there was a second deer. Fabien volunteered to process his son's deer along with his deer because his son's deer had enabled them to find his deer. This became a 'triple reward' when Fabien shared the deer meat with his friend's family. It is when we go to help another, that the Lord is actually able to provide us with what we need. It is our concern for the needs of each other, and the very action taken by us to help them, that allows all of us to experience God's priceless promises.

Chapter 6

Gain True Happiness

If a man therefore purge himself from these, he shall be a vessel of honor unto the Lord, sanctified and meet for the Master's use, and prepared unto every good work.

2 Timothy 2:21

The Lord's desire is that we 'Come' unto Him 'just as we are' and to keep our focus on Him and to not worry what people think. This requires that we 'lean not unto our own understanding' (Proverbs 3:5) and be willing to live our lives as Jesus did, "Not my will but Thy will be done" (Luke 22:42). Our journey walking in obedience to the leading of the Lord's Holy Spirit, contains a lot of contrasts, for we are instructed, "Love not the world, nor the things that are in the world' (1 John 3:15).

Blessings

The way of this world is to desire to gain happiness from obtaining the 'things' of the world without implementation or regard for the truths contained in the Bible; but the true blessings that come from the Lord, come as a 'result' of living yielded and obedient to His Commandments. Blessings are a result, not a goal.

Freedom

The way of this world is to seek happiness from 'freedom' to do whatever we desire; but the Lord gives real freedom to those who follow Him in His steps. It is His presence 'within us' that brings us not only 'true happiness' but also 'great joy'!

The message from this world is for us to embrace non-conforming individuality; but the Lord seeks to magnify Himself through each of us 'individually' using the talents and gifts that each of us have been given for His glory and honor.

Truth

The message from the world is that there is 'no' truth and that each person has the right to choose how to live their life, that no one has the right to tell anyone else what to do; but the message of the Lord Jesus Christ is:
"I am the way, the truth, and the life, no man cometh unto the Father but by me" (John 14:6).

God's Holy Spirit

There are unclean spirits in this world which seek to create fear out of chaos, rather than faith on earth. Believers are given His Holy Spirit and instructed: 'ye have received the spirit of adoption whereby we cry Abba Father' (Romans 8:15).

Service

The world remains focused on the things of this world and the cares of this world. Believers are told to focus on service to the Lord and on duty to one another, and allow the Lord to meet all of our needs "according to His riches in glory by Christ Jesus" (Philippians 4:19-21).

Time

The world seeks to have us use our time focused on things that can be done in this material world. Believers are to focus on eternity and on the eternal souls of men, who need to hear the promises of the Lord, and on His assurances that He IS in control even when things are happening that appear to be 'very bad', His promise is to work all for our good (Romans 8:28).

Praise

The way of the world is to seek the praise of men, to climb the ladder of success, and to be admired by others. Believers are told to seek only praise from the Lord which is invisible, and to expect persecution and misunderstandings. Believers are told to give whatever praise men give us to the Lord for His working in and through us!

Access to God

There are many ways that people work to obtain access to the spiritual world. The use of meditation, repeating words of affirmation, and being careful to think only 'good' thoughts are just a few. Believers are told to pray to God, to read His Bible, and to commit to memory the promises contained within the word of God. His promise is that His word will not return VOID, and that through it we can 'quench all the fiery darts of the wicked' (Ephesians 6:16).

Jesus

The world tells us that Jesus was just a good man, that He was NOT the Son of God, and that there are many ways to reach God. These include the messages of Ghandi, Buddha, Mohammad, and Jesus, and it matters not which path one takes, all paths lead to God. The Bible assures us that Jesus said, "I am the way, the truth, and the life, no man cometh to the Father but by me' (John 14:6). It is true that while on this earth, we may travel north, south, east or west. But access to God is provided to us on His terms: "My thoughts are not your thoughts, neither are my ways your ways, saith the Lord. As the heavens are higher than the earth, so are my ways higher than your ways, and my thoughts than your thoughts, saith the Lord" (Isaiah 55-8-10). We are commanded to look to Jesus. "Looking unto Jesus the author and finisher of our faith, who for the joy that was set before him, endured the cross, despising the shame, and is set down on the right hand of the throne of God' (Hebrews 12:2).

"And Jesus came and said, "All power is given unto me, in heaven and on earth" (Matthew 28:18).

Chapter 7

Find Real Love

No man can serve two masters; for either he will hate the one, and love the other; or else he will hold to the one and despise the other. Ye cannot serve God and mammon.
Matthew 6:24

One of the biggest challenges in our lives is to really show our love for one another. It is easy to say that we care, but it is much more challenging to actually step up and do the things that 'love' would do for one another. Those opportunities are all around us. The problem is that we do not have 'eyes to see' those opportunities, and when we do see them, it is quite easy to 'walk away' and trust that someone else will handle things. Each opportunity that arrives, often requires not just ourselves, but many people to rise and be there to help one another, even someone who is a total stranger.

A Need Fulfilled

My husband Fabien has done an amazing job creating his 'work shop' in the garage. One thing he wanted, was a small refrigerator. He searched on the web sites for a 'deal' and found a small fridge for sale for $50 in the next town. He called and it was available, so off we went with his truck to pick up that fridge.

When we arrived, an older woman greeted us at the door. She told us, "I am moving, and there are other things that need to go as well." As Fabien visited, I began to pray for this woman and ask the Lord to help her with the move that was obviously going to be a big job. As we walked through the home, I noticed a framed picture on the wall, and said, "This is a beautiful picture of yellow tulips!" She replied, "Yes, my daughter got that picture for me. When my husband was alive, he purchased yellow roses for me all the time. Once he passed, my daughter gave me that picture of yellow tulips. They are not the right kind of flower, but I still love the picture because it reminds me of my husband!" Fabien paid her for the fridge. As we left, she suggested he look in the garage for perhaps something else he might want to purchase. Fabien did enter the garage and looked, but the things he was interested in, she was taking with her when she moved. Before he left, she said, "Here is a chainsaw that does not work that I am happy to give to you if you want it, because it has to go!" Fabien said, "Sure, I can take it off your hands, maybe I can fix it!" Once we were home, Fabien made a project out of it, and he was able with a lot of effort to get it running.

An Opportunity to Show Love

The next time I was in town to assist my blind friend with getting groceries, I had to use the bathroom as we were checking out. When I left to get to the restroom, I had to walk past the flower shop in the store, and as I passed, I noticed they had a bunch of 'yellow roses' for sale. The roses were more than I wanted to pay, but as I remembered our visit and that older woman, I bought a bundle of them for her as a 'thank you' for the chainsaw. I would drop them off to the woman on my way home.

When I knocked at the door, she came and was surprised by the gift of yellow roses. I said, "If you have a vase, I will arrange them for you!" She replied, "I do have a vase!" I followed her into her kitchen and as I worked to put them in her vase, she shared with me what was happening. She had just 30 days to move and did not know how she could manage. She was disabled and her family was out-of-state, and she had no one to help her with any of it. I listened. When she finished talking, I said, "I have friends in two different churches, that would likely be able to provide people who could come and assist you, would you like me to check with them?" She replied, "Yes, that would be great!" I realized as we talked, that what she really needed was someone like me, who understood the logistics of organization, and who had the ability to arrange and stage the move. Then very spontaneously, I said, "I myself, have organized and managed major projects for a University and I can come and help you organize this move, I will be back tomorrow."

A Daunting Task

Once home I contacted friends in both churches, and other friends of mine. People were committing themselves to come and help me pack boxes for her, and bring them to Good Will. Her basement was well organized, but it contained many, many shelves: wall to wall shelves on one side, and those shelves were full of the accumulations of life!

Day after day, people would meet and work with her to sort and box. Each day I picked up and brought empty boxes for us to fill. Each afternoon when I left, I would pack my car with filled boxes that then were brought to Good Will.

I could tell she was not eating properly, so on my way home, I would call and ask her if she would like me to pick up something for her to eat on my way back to her home. She would thank me and tell me what to pick up for her and I would bring it to her. Each time we would agree on what area to work on the next day. We went through the home, each room, kitchen, living room, bedrooms, bathrooms, and closets, including the basement. Room by room was packed in boxes, and each box was carefully taped and marked to identify what was inside and from which room it would need to be placed for her new home. The 'to keep' boxes were stacked in the corner of her living room for the movers to bring to her new location.

Because of my concern for her health, each day we would limit the time we worked, but each day we got a lot accomplished. She continued to post and sell what she could sell. She had a friend who agreed to come with a truck to remove metal from an outdoor garage area and he came and took what she had. Sometimes it seemed like it would never get done, and I would pray to the Lord for His help and strength to finish in time for the closing of the home. The buyers would do a walk through and the home needed to be ready for the new purchaser's walk through. I encouraged her and said, "The Lord will help us to get things together and finished in time."

A Clean Up Team

She had a close friend who was a neighbor who came every day to help as well. Her friend L. was a total example of 'love' and had an incredible attitude, and her love for her neighbor was more than words. L. and I agreed to be the 'clean up' team for vacuuming and wiping things down once the home was emptied by the movers of all the furniture. The plan was for me to bring my vacuum from my home on that last day. The woman who was moving would do the closing and head to her new home the morning that the movers left.

The Trip

Finally, we came to what I thought was the end. My husband Fabien, had agreed to use his truck and trailer to bring a load of what she was keeping from the garage to her new location in the next State. As she showed him what needed to be moved, he made his assessment of what would fit on his truck and what weight his trailer could carry.

He would bring her lawn mower, a work bench, table, and other items she wanted moved. When we finished agreeing on what would go on his truck and trailer, as we stood in her garage, Fabien looked up. We both looked up as well to see what he was looking at. He said, "There is a pull-down door right there! What is up there?"

She looked at us and put her hand over her head! There are things up there as well, she exclaimed! Fabien pulled the door down and went up to look. He used his phone flashlight. Unbelievably, she was able to pull herself up the ladder and follow him up to see what had been stored above the garage area. Fabien and her looked at the things together. There was another whole room full of things that needed to be moved!

Once she was up the ladder, she needed assistance getting back down! Fabien carefully maneuvered himself down the ladder to help her back down the ladder. She was very grateful.

She had been able to get an organization to come and pick up boxes that we packed and stacked in her garage. Some of the boxes they would not take, and those had to be transported to Good Will.

Church Help!

The Pastor of Northside Baptist Church, agreed to send a deacon who had a truck to remove the items above the garage and place them in their annual free garage 'sale' which took no money, but just gave the items to people who came to pick them up on the day set aside for this event. Finally, a week prior to the Northside church free day, the church allowed boxes for the free day in their basement, so I brought things there rather than to Good Will. Amazingly one of the items the woman had determined could go, she decided she wanted back. Because it was at the church, I was able to go back to the church and bring that item back to her.

During the move, I continually told her that I was there to help her with the move. She offered for me to take whatever I wanted, but I exclaimed, "I do NOT want anything! When this is done, I am going to go through all my things and do the same thing!" When we were through, that is EXACTLY what Fabien and I did, which included giving away to Habitat a caricature picture of him on a tractor!

Deemed Unredeemable

The one thing that no one would take was outdoor chairs that were on her back lawn. Those would need to go to the dump. Good Will and Habitat did not want them. Fabien came with his truck to remove those outdoor chairs for her and they were brought to our home so we could bring them to the dump. I told Fabien, "Maybe they can be cleaned." He had his doubts. But the next day, I went with a bottle of Tilex and hosed them with water and sprayed them. As I finished spraying the last chair, I thought to myself. 'What I am doing! This is such a waste of time!' The chairs were black. They did not look like anything could be done to save them. But to my 'shock and awe' when I turned around and looked back at the first chair I had sprayed, it had turned almost 'white' before my eyes. Fabien came out of our home at that very moment and exclaimed, "Well you really must have scrubbed on them to get them that clean!" I said, "No, all I did was spray them with this!" as I held up the Tilex bottle!

Those chairs are a perfect example of the Lord's ability to 'redeem, recovery, and restore' us to Himself, no matter what our life has been, no matter what 'messes' we have gotten into, the Lord is able to 'save' us from living 'wasted lives' and change our stony hearts!

"A new heart also will I give you, and a new Spirit will I put within you; and I will take the stony heart out of your flesh, and I will give you a heart of flesh (Ezekiel 36:26).

The Surprise

When the final day came for Fabien to load his truck and trailer with those things that needed to go with her to her new home, we went and loaded everything and brought the trailer back to our home for the night. The woman had an outdoor table cart and an outdoor chair and a bench that had been used to sit on outside during the process of moving things. Once the trailer was in my yard, I removed the bench and the chair and the serving cart, and sprayed all three with Tilex. Each of them also turned 'white' before my eyes. After they were all clean, I re-loaded them back onto the trailer for our trip to her new home.

Once we arrived, and unloaded the trailer, she asked, "Where did this chair come from?" I replied, "This is that chair I was sitting on during the move, the one that was black!" She said, "It cannot be that chair!" I told her, "I know! But it is THAT chair!" Then, I unloaded her outdoor cart, and her bench. I said, "It is just amazing that all three cleaned right up!" She smiled! She was just as amazed as we were.

The Bells

During the packing, the woman had boxes full of bells that she asked me to take to Good Will. The boxes were too heavy for me to lift, so I had asked Fabien to come and help me with that last load to bring the boxes up out of the basement to Good Will. When he learned that the boxes contained bells, he said, "I would like the boxes of bells, can I have them?" The woman agreed he could have them. I replied, "Whatever do you want them for?" He replied, "I don't know, I would just like to look at them." Reluctantly I agreed to allow him to take the boxes of bells to our home. I was NOT excited about the decision at all. We wanted to clean out our garage and now we would be adding two boxes to our garage area. Once home he unloaded the two boxes and placed one on top of the other in the front area of one garage bay. I thought to myself, "Well, let's just open one of these boxes and see." I opened the top box, and pulled out one bell and looked at it. To my utter surprise the very bell that I pulled out had a 'Hippopotamus' on it! It was a bell from Granby Quebec's Zoo! That was the only bell that was inside those two boxes of bells that had a hippo on it. For me that 'hippo bell' was a token to me from the Lord that what I had done for this woman was 'pleasing in the Lord's sight'. Had Fabien not insisted we take the boxes of those bells, and had he not placed the right box on top of the other, and had I not been inclined to open the box to see, I would not have found that 'hippo bell.' To me, the value of the bell was its spiritual currency. I knew that the Lord had answered our prayers and had helped us! For 30 days, the Lord had provided volunteers who made it possible for this woman to meet the deadline for her closing and for her move.

"Pure religion and undefiled before God and the Father is this, to visit the widows and the fatherless in their affliction and to keep himself unspotted from the world" (James 1:27).

The Gift of Service

The entire month as well as our trip with the truck and trailer to drop off and meet our new friend in her new home was a great undertaking for a complete stranger. The trip alone took several hours for us, there and back. The day of our trip I brought the cooler packed with a lunch for all of us. After our truck and trailer were unloaded, we sat in her new garage on folding chairs and enjoyed 'egg salad' sandwiches and drinks. We enjoyed her company, and I rejoiced that the Lord had given us the opportunity to help her in her time of need. Receiving help is also a challenge. This move was not easy and required facing many lifetime memories attached to items that needed to have new homes. Her ability to 'let go' and move on is a lesson for all of us to value people – for in the end we can take nothing with us to heaven. May the Lord continue to provide this woman with His special angels to watch over her, and provide people with hearts of flesh to assist her with her needs!

"And whosoever doth not bear his cross, and come after me, cannot be my disciple. For which of you, intending to build a tower, sitteth not down first, and counteth the cost, whether he hath sufficient to finish it. (Luke 14:27-28).

Chapter 8

Be Thankful

And let the peace of God rule in your hearts, to which ye were called unto one body; and be ye also Thankful.

Colossians 3:15

We are told that the way to enter the presence of the Lord is with 'thankfulness' and into his courts with 'praise'. "Enter His gates with thanksgiving and courts with praise: be thankful unto him, and bless his name" (Psalm 100:4).

One of the best ways to become 'thankful' is to be willing to serve one another. My own service would include something that I had not had any desire to be involved in doing. When I was married to my first husband, Jim, he had decided to go from an engineering position to become a law enforcement officer, a policeman. His decision would lead him to the role of Sargent and then a Detective. There were some individuals who ended up in jail as a result of the testimony of my first husband. I actually received a threatening call from someone who really disliked my husband when my husband was at work and I was home alone. This caused my first husband to sleep with a gun under his pillow. We also had a security system installed in our home. That meant we could not open doors or windows without entering a code to turn it off and then turn it back on. This was the only way he felt more secure when he was not home after the threatening call.

We both were members of the Faith Baptist Church and that church had a prison ministry. We both were asked to become a part of that ministry of visiting the prisons. But he and I were not up to the challenge. It seemed bizarre to me then that we would be asked to do that, when we were part of the process that caused individuals to be put into prison. I could not get my head around it, but it seemed to make logical sense to those involved in the ministry to have my husband the police officer and his wife visiting those in prison. My attitude was not one of 'thankfulness' for the opportunity and I was glad when Jim, my first husband, refused and asked me not to get involved as well. We did not disclose to anyone that we had been threatened. He worked with his Police Department about the threat and we went on with our lives.

What we did attempt to do, was to care for my mother before she passed, but her care was too involved for either of us to handle and although we were both willing to try to have her live with us, my family ended up having her placed in a home for those with needs, and then I would go to visit her there. She is now with the Lord.

My thankfulness to the Lord was for His not giving us more than we could bear (1 Corinthians 10:13).

A Second Opportunity to Serve

It would take 25 years before the door would open for me to be involved with those in prison, through a request for me to write to someone in prison. This opportunity to write to someone would bring great joy. Each week I write a letter and there are now 5 years of weekly letters.

This person is very similar to Joseph who was falsely accused and who ended up in prison. Because this person would not agree to admit to doing something that had NOT been done with a plea agreement, the court gave a maximum sentence of 30 years. An immediate appeal process was begun, but the first appeal was denied for a technicality, and the second appeal was also denied. The ironic part of these denials is that both appeals had to go to the very same judge that placed the man in prison to begin with. This also made no sense to me. Why would a ruling judge, who had the opportunity to see the same case again, rule against his own ruling? Another appeal is in the works but this is a very slow process bringing this case into its 8th year.

Added Opportunities

My present husband Fabien and I went to visit the man and my husband Fabien realized that he knew him.

My letters have been well received and others have written to me and asked me to write to them. So, I began to write to each person who wrote to me as well. When one of my Christian friends found out I was writing to someone in prison, I was asked to write to someone else. So, my letters now go to several prisons in several different states.

When my close friend Becky learned I was writing she asked me to send the letters to her, and when she gets each letter, she reads the letter to her friends that are in the Home where she lives. So, the weekly letter now goes to many, many individuals, via mail, and email. One of the individuals in prison wrote recently that he reads the letter to his roommate, and now every week that roommate asks, "Did the letter come yet for the week?" The letter does not take much time for me to write, but it does impact a lot of different people helping each of us to be grateful to the Lord for His comfort during trials.

One of the Letters

DATE Hi (name)

One of Fabien's son's went to Ohio on a deer hunt and posted a picture of his 9 pointer yesterday. He is a very happy man for sure! His other son is working to harvest his first crop of hemp which is a lot of work trimming the plants and capturing the buds. Bruce and Sharon Paterson from Northside Baptist Church reported their Philippines trip, so far, is accomplishing its mission and purpose, to encourage those in devasted areas to have hope and to know that people care for them in the USA. Truly this world is full of difficult situations that challenge our faith to believe that the Lord will actually work ALL things together for our good in His time. Believers are following a very long line of individual believers who have gone before us, who have been put to the 'test' and who have 'passed' the test. Abraham with his son Isaac, willing to offer him up not knowing the Lord would intervene with an angel to stop him; Joseph enduring dreadful days in prison for something he was accused of doing that he did not do, which took many years for the Lord to turn things around. It is hard to remember that this world is 'temporary' and the real purpose of everything is for 'eternal' ends that we cannot yet see or even truly comprehend.

What we are promised from the Lord is that He will give us the strength we need in measure for each day- but we MUST ask for it! Like the song: 'One by one, the days the moments fleeting, til we reach the promised land.' When we connect with the Lord through prayer, we can know that 'The Lord is nigh, is mightier than the noise of many waters, yea then the mighty waves of the sea' (Psalm 93:4). Fabien visited a BMW dealership this week, and said he never felt so uncomfortable in his life. He felt overwhelmed with the luxuries in the place. We talked about his visit afterward being very much like the end of this life. Death is the mighty force that will level all of us. Each of us will give an account of our life, and 'to whom much is given- much shall be required'. We talked about the day Jesus was in the Temple and observed an older woman putting in 'two pence' and another man giving a large gift, but the Lord exclaimed that the older woman had given more than everyone for she had given 'all she had' and others had given 'of the abundance of what they had.' It is good for us to remember that the Lord does not look on the outward appearance but on the deeper things of the heart.

Yesterday, Fabien and I went with the truck to see a table and 4 chairs that looked like it would match for our current table. The chairs were just a bit darker color but exactly the same style, and we got them for a very good price. I had been asking the Lord for 4 more chairs that would match our current table, because I absolutely did not want to purchase another table set. We have been having 7 people when I host the dinner, I didn't have enough chairs for everyone. That required us to use my computer chair, our rocking chair and Fabien's desk chair from the porch. Now we have as many as 9 chairs, so we no longer have to bring our 'odd chairs' to the table. Praise His Holy Name!

The Northside bible reading was from Acts about Saul's encounter with the Lord being knocked down to the earth, he seeing a man, and asking, "Who art thou?" The Lord replied, "I am Jesus whom though art persecuting!" The Pastor pointed out that Saul was working to please a God that he did not know by following his religion! Saul's conversion to

"Paul" is like our own conversion process. We must get our own reality check. We must become willing to change, and to be willing to follow a different path. To do that, we must have FAITH – in what is NOT seen, and that requires that we be willing to look up to God for His help! ↑ dawn

---

I always sign my name with an arrow pointing up to heaven.

The opportunities for each of us to be part of one another abound. Truly the harvest is plentiful but the laborers are few (Matthew 9:37). The reality is that in one moment, we could be on the other side in heaven. The challenge is for us to live our days with eternity in mind. This viewpoint helps us to be thankful and to be willing to be there for each other. And the Lord has promised to, 'reward those who diligently seek Him' (Hebrews 11:6).

Chapter 9

Praise Him!

While I live, I will praise the Lord!
I will sing praises unto my God while I have any being.

Psalm 146:1

The question asked by my friend Nancy on a recent visit was, "Whatever are you doing?" I replied, "Whatever are you talking about?"

She said, 'You wait right here, I have something for you!" Then she disappeared to another room. When she returned, she had a gallon container in her hand. I said, "Oh, you have 'maple syrup," for me??" She replied, "It's not maple syrup! It's the shampoo that you love, a whole gallon of it!" I gasped, "What! I just cancelled an order for that yesterday, because it is way too expensive!" My head spun around at the sight of the gift! It was a salon sized contained of very expensive shampoo, most likely worth over $500.

My friendship with Nancy spans over 45 years and each of us had been through a lot of life's trials, and we still face trials.

Every month, another lifelong friend Sue travels to meet me and we ride together to Nancy's home. We try to meet monthly to have fellowship and to enjoy our friendship and make prayer lists for the month. Sue and I had just discussed with Sue as we traveled to Nancy's home the blessings of the Lord, and how the Lord often provides unusual events that empower us to be able to 'get through' difficult times. I had explained, "The Lord can bless us and answer our prayers; it is not for us to try to understand how the Lord works, it is ours to Praise His Holy Name!"

Now here was one of my prayers being answered in a very large way. I told them, "Well I just told the Lord I would have to find a different shampoo for my hair, because I want to spend my money on missions and on supporting the church. I even told him I would use every last ounce of what I had, and stretch it as far as I could by using less! Now, here I will have enough for several years!" Sue exclaimed, "Had this been a regular size, I would have accounted it to coincidence, but I just can't do that with a container that size, and the fact that Nancy won it, is just amazing, Truly, this is an answered prayer from the Lord!"

Stand

We enjoyed our visit and updated one another with our prayer requests. Our discussion included the reality that each of us can be misunderstood by those who love the Lord. My own experience has been when unexplainable answers to prayer occur, the door is opened for others to question such an experience. Often it can be a challenge for us to give the Lord the Praise that IS due His holy name! When that happens within my being, all I want to do is to 'run' rather than to be 'judged'.

On the way home in Sue's car, a wild bunny darted in front of her car. She was able to miss hitting it, and the car that we met was able to miss hitting it as well. The verse, "Watch ye, stand fast in the faith, quick you like men, be strong" (1 Corinthians 16:30) flashed through my mind.

I silently prayed to the Lord that He would help me to 'stand fast' and not run like the bunny away from conversations that can be sometimes difficult because there is rarely an answer to "why" the Lord does the things that he does. And clearly running contains dangers of its own, like Peter who denied Christ 3 times, we must be willing not only to Praise Him, but to not deny the work He is doing in our life!

Fasting, Prayer and Praise

One of the most rewarding ways believers are able to offer true praise to the Lord, is by combining three different areas through fasting, praying and praising the Lord. When done in unison with purpose, and focus, the resulting connection and awareness of the Lord's loving care pours into our lives in the most extraordinary ways.

My interest in doing a Daniel 21 day fast began when I learned of Jentezen Franklin's experiences with fasting. His book "Fasting" covers experiences that have occurred as a result of dedicated fasting. The fast begins with three days of liquids only, and then moves into eating just fruits and vegetables, and nuts with chicken broth. Preparing our hearts by prayer before fasting is critical. Once a decision has been made to fast, just jump in and do it. Focus on just one day at a time, and keep a regular Bible study, journal, and prayer time, but add to all of that as much praise as possible, especially when you are feeling tired, deprived and hungry!

Each time I have done a fast the Lord has blessed me with answered prayers and confirmations of his presence, love and care. The process creates a union between the Lord, you and others, and that union continues even after the fast. It also fuels each prayer for those for whom you pray. It is important to have a list of the things that you would like answers for, as well as the needs of those you love who are struggling. Make a point to pray for everyone and for those things on your list as many times a day as you think of them. Set aside time as well in the morning, evening and during the day, to pull out the list and lift their names up to the Lord.

My prayer below, is what I say to the Lord for each person, including myself:

Lord, please hear my prayer and honor me for honoring you with this fast. Thank you for helping me to do this fast, and to keep me on track. Help me Lord to see what you want me to see, and to do those things that you would have me do – today! Be with those that I love and help them!

Cover (name of person) Lord with your precious blood, and in the name of Jesus Christ, I rebuke the power of the enemy in their lives, and ask that you through your precious blood bring their thoughts into captivity to the Lord Jesus Christ that your name might be glorified and honored. Give them mental clarity, physical health and strength and emotional stability and protect them and keep them by the power of your Holy Spirit. Send you angels to guide, lead and help them, I ask this in the precious name of Jesus Christ, that YOUR NAME may receive the honor and glory due throughout all eternity as a result of this prayer this day. **Lord, forgive us,**

have mercy on us, and help us!

Intervene *with your power for your name's sake, and for the sake of this prayer.*

Deliver *us Lord from the lusts of the flesh, the lusts of the eye, the pride of life and the love of this world.*

Redeem *us through your shed blood and give us fellowship with you.*

Restore *us through your Holy Spirit. Restore our relationships – one with another, and give us your mercy and grace.*

Recover *us from the snares of the enemy who seeks to keep us from the best that you have for us, by diversion and distraction and help us to give you the glory and honor due your Holy Name!*

Day 1 and Day 21 – Answered Prayers

It is typical for the Lord to provide confirmation on the first day as well as on Day 21 of fasts, with tangible answers. During my most recent fast, one of my requests to the Lord was to help me finish this book. My own doubts of the need to write it, as well as my desire to know if the Lord really wanted me to work to finish it, circled in my head. My desire to live a private life, and my concern for 'what will people think' caused me to come to a roaring stop. I prayed to the Lord to guide and lead me. On Day 21 of my fast, I received a letter from an individual I had been asked to write to, who was back in a facility for making an impulsive decision that did not serve him well. *Who has not done that?!* He asked for a copy of my second book, "Experiencing God's Amazing Ways' and I mailed him a copy. Below is his letter.

Dawn,

It was nice to receive your letter the other day. Made me smile and filled my day with joy and happiness. Like always! So, the reason I'm sitting down and writing you at this moment is I have something really cool to tell you!!! So, everyone that wanted to read your book has read it and the last person finished it last night. I wanted everyone here who wanted to, to get to read it first because this is 'reception' and I can get moved any day. So, I figured it was smart to let others read it first, because the book will come with me when I leave. I started reading it this morning. After dinner, I was talking to my buddy about how I kind of gave up on God over the years and was mad at him because of my own actions and everything I've been through: loosing my family, being in and out of prison, missing so much of my daughter's life, etc. Well shortly after we had our little talk, I picked up your book and started reading it again. At the end of Chapter 7: Consecration, page 46, you had 4 questions that amazed me and after this letter I want to answer them on paper so I have a nice reminder. The questions went as follows:

1. *Can we actually praise the Lord even when things are not going our way?*
2. *Will we believe in God even when bad things are happening to us?*
3. *Will we trust Him to intervene in answer to our prayers on behalf*

of ourselves and others?

*It is during this life that we have the opportunity to bring glory to the Lord in the midst of trials."

That goes hand-in-hand with what we were talking 20 minutes earlier about! God is Awesome All the time! Thought you would enjoy that, so I had to write you!

Till pen meets paper – God bless, (signature)

My letter back to him is below:

Dear (name),
Thank you for sharing my book with those you are with and for letting me know about your conversation with your friend and how that conversation dovetailed to page 46 just 20 minutes later. God is INDEED Awesome – ALL THE TIME!!! When I was at the P.O. getting the mail and your letter, I met someone that I knew from riding the CCV bus to UVM. The man spoke with me and as we walked outside, he exclaimed, "I am really a very PRIVATE person, and don't usually talk with anyone!" I told him I had something for him and that it contained a lot of my very own private information which I felt awkward sharing, because of 'shame' and 'fear of what people would think' but that I had determined that we all someday will give an account to the Lord, and if something could be 'gained' to help others with similar issues, it was worth my disclosure, because then the Lord could use those things for healing for 'me' and 'others'.

So, your letter was a bit of an 'answered prayer' for me. I am now just finishing up my 3rd book, "Experiencing God's Priceless, Precious, Promises," and my question to the Lord yesterday was, "Is it worth the time and effort it takes to do this? Because what difference does it make?" My goal in writing books, is not to 'draw attention to myself' but rather to encourage people to 'turn to the Lord' and to PRAY serious prayers, from their heart. Prayers are not just words. Once we ask the Lord, we need to THEN WAIT for the Lord to answer as well as be okay if that answer is "NO" or "WAIT" or "NOT NOW." My BIGGEST dilemma becoming 'SAVED' was that I was convinced I already HAD a relationship with God. I was so sure of that, that I did not believe I had to go to Jesus for forgiveness, or to save my soul, because I was 'all set'. Now I encourage everyone to MAKE SURE (that these words come out of your mouth (out load) and that you mean what you say with all your heart. . . because that is EXACTLY where miracles begin and where a 'peace' beyond our ability to understand starts, no matter where we are or what has happened to us): *"Lord Jesus, I do believe you came, you died, and that you rose again. I know that I have made mistakes and I ask you to forgive me and remember me when I come into your Kingdom. Come into my Heart and save my soul, and help me to follow you!"* From that point forward, God gives an inner awareness that "I am NOT alone anymore!" Praise His Holy Name that Jesus comes to us 'right where we are' and starts right there. And He promises to NEVER leave nor forsake us!

I encourage you to read the Bible – a KJV version if you can. The gospel of John is enclosed. If I have sent this to you before, please share it with someone you feel lead to give it to. The words in the Bible have God's

Holy SPIRIT in them and LIFE. They are like SEEDS in our MINDS that get planted that the Lord uses down the road when we least expect it. I am unsure if you have any experience with 'FASTING' and PRAYING and PRAISING but these three things when done 'TOGETHER" for the right REASON are a 3- fold CORD connection to God that is not easily broken. We FAST not to RECEIVE anything but solely to 'block out' distractions so we can connect with the Lord in a powerful way. One thing that Jesus asked us to pray for is "for laborers for His harvest" and that is one of my prayers to the Lord. My questions to you are:

What is your life going to be in the end when you give an account?

What will you have to give to the Lord when you meet him?

Why not choose to give your 'self' to HIM, and ask Him to help you to become a 'vessel' for His use?

Then have an attitude of GRATITUDE as you begin to be willing and ready to do WHATEVER he has for you to do. Start every day with reading something from the Bible. Then ask Jesus to help you to make the right decisions. Pray about those things that are happening! Be willing to 'give up' YOUR will to seek HIS will. This is what Jesus meant when he promised us 'life" more abundant! God seeks those who will trust, and walk by FAITH and not by SIGHT. And begin to give glory to God in all that you say, and do. Jesus is calling your name – can you hear Him? I am praying the Lord will open a door for you for your 'next' location, and that you will become a 'laborer' for the Lord, and able to participate in a Bible study with others who are just like me and you- willing to learn!

Look up! dawn ↑

---[end of my letter]

God's Plan

We all belong to God and each of us has been given a free will choice. The Lord has revealed just enough of himself to us through His creation and nature, and through the promises contained within the pages of the Bible, to provide us with enough reasonable information for us to exercise an act of faith. God has not provided us with total 'revelation' of all of His mysteries, for if He did, our 'free will' choice would become more of our very definite choice, that would guarantee that we did not miss out on his blessings to come. Knowing all about God's provisions would remove our ability to exercise true faith. By revealing too much of Himself to us while we are still in fleshly bodies, we would then be more focused on what we will receive from Him someday, as well as what He is able to do for us right now in this lifetime. Our focus would be twisted towards us, rather than towards Him where we can bring Him the glory due His name.

God sent His only begotten Son, Jesus Christ to the earth to live a perfect life, and then allowed men to nail Him to a cross. Jesus prayed, 'not my will but Thine be done." Jesus was nailed to a cross and physically died, and then God raised Him back to life eternal. Angels rolled the huge stone away, and told the woman who came to anoint the body, "He is not here, He is risen!" Jesus then appeared first to Mary who lingered at the tomb, and then to the apostles and finally to 500 before a cloud circled His feet and he was lifted up from earth into heaven on the Mount of Olives. As Jesus was taken off the earth He proclaimed, "All power is given unto me in heaven and on earth." He gave the great commission to 'Go' and a reminder "Lo, I am with you always even to the end of the world." (Matthew 28: 18-20)

We have a free gift of salvation through Jesus Christ's sacrifice on our behalf. Our 'verbal commitment' to Jesus is like a wedding vow.

When we trust God and the work of Jesus to forgive us for the wrongs we have done, God saves our eternal soul. I came very close to living a very different life with my own self sufficiency doing what I believed to be right. It was God who opened a door for me to see that I did need His mercy and forgiveness.

I did not hear about God's plan of salvation through Jesus Christ until I was 23 years old. I was born into the denomination of my family. I went to church, I was baptized as a baby, I had a first communion, and then did religious acts. This 'inoculated' me into believing all was well, when all was not well. All these outward actions attempt something that God has already done for us. "Not by works of righteousness that we have done, but by His mercy He saved us, by the washing and regeneration and renewing of the Holy Ghost which he shed on us abundantly through Jesus Christ our Savior" (Titus 3:5-7).

Lord, we praise you and thank you, for doing all the work for us, and allowing us to just 'come' and learn of you, because your yoke is 'easy' and your burden is 'light'! (Matthew 16: 28-30

Chapter 10

Be Ready Always

But sanctify the Lord God in your hearts, and be ready always to give an answer to every man that asketh you a reason of the hope that is in you with meekness and fear.

1 Peter 3:15

My bi-weekly trip to visit with my friend who is blind would involve asking an unusual question. My trip this day would include the Lord's Holy Spirit impressing upon me to ask a question: "Would it be easier for an atheist, or for an agnostic to come to faith?" My reply to the Lord was, "I am willing to ask the question, but how I ask this question, and the time of when I ask this question, as well as the way in which I present the question, is important, so I will wait for you to open that door!"

We enjoyed visiting and getting groceries, and as we left the grocery store, I remembered that the Holy Spirit had asked me to ask the question. Again, I prayed to the Lord, "Please let me know when the right time is to ask this question!" I then literally moved the question out of my mind.

When groceries were unloaded, after we visited as I got up to leave, suddenly I remembered that I must ask the question. I sat back down, and said, "Oh, I remember now, I wanted to ask you your opinion on something I was pondering on my trip this morning. I have my own opinion, but I am very interested to know what your thoughts are on this.

Would it be easier for an atheist or for an agnostic to come to faith? I believe that it would be harder for an atheist to come to faith, what do you think?" My blind friend replied, "That is an easy answer, it would be the atheist, as the atheist does not believe, so I agree with your answer." Just then her friend came into the kitchen area. Her friend had also heard the question and said, "And I agree, too! I am an atheist, really an 'agnostic atheist' and I live my life as I want because there is just not enough evidence to proof that God exists." I replied, "I really appreciate your answer. I have never heard of an 'agnostic atheist' before."

I said, "My husband and I just finished watching a DVD about an atheist. Charles Templeton who started work with Billy Graham and soon after left his faith entirely and became an atheist. The DVD was done by Lee Strobel, a former legal reporter for the Chicago Tribune who also was an atheist. You might enjoy that DVD." A discussion followed whether they could even play a DVD. I added, "I certainly do not want to bring anything that you would not be interested in watching!" But he replied, "Yes, bring it, I can play it on my computer."

So later that week, I dropped of the DVD package with 3 DVDS from Lee Strobel: The Case for Faith, The Case for Christ, and The Case for Creation.

My blind friend asked, "Who is actually on these DVD's?" I replied, "Lee Strobel, Charles Templeton and professors from different universities around the world that are interviewed." My goal with all of this was obedience only to the leading of God's Holy Spirit, not anything more.

The truth is that unless the Lord is able to open our eyes, none of us would be able to have any faith at all. I myself had determined as a teenager that "Jesus Christ" did not have anything to do with anything. My assessment was that everything was based on thoughts and 'thoughts produced things' and therefore controlling our thoughts was important. It is only by the grace of God that I was granted the ability to have faith and to trust in what is written in the Bible about Jesus.

My conclusion after reading the bible, was that it HAD to be true, and if it WAS true, the whole meaning of life was really outside of the physical realm. That insight opened a door for me to pray and accept his gift of His forgiveness, and to ask Him, like that thief, to remember me when I come into His Kingdom.

Since that time, I was one of the care providers for an atheist who was the head of a major hospital, who has since passed. The first day we met, he asked me what I believed. He insisted, I answer his question. I told him, "I believe in the man who walked through walls!" His initial response to me was that people within his field would call me "Delusional". But the Lord was able to soften his heart through a minister who visited him and shared hope and the promise of eternal life through faith in Jesus Christ. That left me with an opening to pray with this atheist a week before he died. He smiled as he acknowledged that he did believe that Jesus came, that he died, that he rose from the dead, and then he asked and accepted His forgiveness. We both cried together, and I said, "You be sure to tell Jesus I said Hi!" He replied, "I will do that!"

So, always be ready to share the hope that you have with those that you meet, even though the message is likely to be 'rejected' at the gate. The Lord has promised that His word will not return void.

"So shall my word be that goeth forth out of my mouth, it shall not return unto me void, but it shall accomplish that which I please, and it shall prosper in the thing whereto I sent it. (Isaiah 55:11)

I also was assigned to care for a professor who had lost her legs, as well as her husband, and her special friend all within a month. Her faith was challenged, and we wept together as she explained what had happened.

The night of the day that she died, the Lord's Holy Spirit told me to stop and visit her. She had been nonresponsive all day, but when I entered the room and called her name, her eyes opened. I told her the Lord had sent me to her to tell her that she was going home. She asked when, and I told her 'soon'. I then told her I was told to ask her if she had lost her faith, and she replied, "I have not!" I said then I am here to pray with you to the Lord to acknowledge that faith in Jesus and His work on the cross, to ask for His forgiveness and for Him to remember you when you come into His Kingdom. She said that prayer, and when she was done, I asked her to tell Jesus that I said hello, when she met him, and she replied, "I can do that!"

What is missing is 'laborers for His Harvest'. Jesus asked us to pray for one thing, "pray ye therefore the Lord of the Harvest, that he would send forth laborers into his harvest" (Matthew 9:38).

Chapter 11

Blessings

If therefore thine eye be single, thy whole body shall be full of light.

Matthew 6:22

Narrower and narrower is our walk with the Lord, until the narrow road has become just a 'line', and this is where God's blessings dwell.

My amazingly 'blessed day" began with having a song in my head called "Providence".

I had got up earlier than normal, to make sure I had time to exercise, have my healthy shake, do my bible reading, pray for the day and make 'bullet points' to help me stay on track. I loaded up my box with my mini animals, and my bag with Bible promise books. As I filled my box, a small dog fell into my hands from my storage container. This dog was ceramic and did not fit in my container for the mini animals, so I placed it within one of the many sleeves of my new purse where I could find it later.

I had to leave early to be on time. I felt bad that I would miss visiting with my sister Treya and her friend Caroline. But as I opened the garage door, Treya and her friend, walked down my driveway and we got to connect and quickly talk about the day. Treya said, "Don't worry about dinner, that will be ready at Audrey's when you get home!" We hugged and I was off!

SEED SOWING

My commitment to the Lord is to give those I meet the love of God and to thank them with Bible promise books and my mini animals. Once I was with my friend, we went and shared a coffee at a restaurant. After our order, I thanked the clerk, with my mini animal and bible book. When we were finished, I went to put our dishes to the bin area, but struggled to locate that area. As I looked for it, a wonderful woman at a table told me where it was located. I placed the dishes in the bin, and turned and thanked her with a mini bear and Bible book. As I turned the corner another woman getting coffee, commented on my fall hat, and I shared another mini animal and bible book with her. When we got to the grocery story, I asked about some veggies we could not locate, and that opened the door for another thank you mini animal, and bible book.

The assistant who waits on us each week, came to tell me she had viewed one of the DVD's "Amazing Grace" and that she was about to watch the DVD on John Newton, the slave trader who wrote the song, "Amazing Grace" which I had given to her as a thank you gift the week before. As we finished talking, I looked to see one of my cousins whom I have not seen in many, many years walking toward us. I asked, "Do you remember me?" Amazingly she did. She had just gotten out of the hospital for a procedure and she was still wearing a hospital bracelet. As we talked, I introduced her to my friend, but they already knew each other. They got to talk and get caught up. Then she gave me information so I could contact her and I told her I would be praying for her. She exclaimed, "It is the Lord that has helped me to get through all of these trials!" The checkout clerk was thanked with a mini animal and Bible book. We headed to the bank and I was able to gift a thank you to the Teller of a mini animal and a bible promise book.

When we were at the grocery store there was something that my friend needed that that store did not carry. So, after I brought her home, I went to another local store to get that item for her. Upon arriving a huge delivery truck was just backing up. I went to tell him how amazing it was that he could back up so easily, and handed him a min animal and bible promise book as I thanked him for doing his job keeping the store stocked. Once in the store, I found the things needed and went to check out. The man in front of me allowed me to put my things on the counter, and I thanked him with a mini bear and bible promise book. The checkout clerk had a sweatshirt with sheep on it, so I thanked her with a mini sheep and bible promise book.

Then I headed off to meet another friend to visit over lunch.

She was running late, which enabled me to thank a UPS truck driver as well as a FedEx driver with mini animals and promise books.

The Small Dog

As I waited for my friend to arrive for lunch, a woman came walking up the street with her dog, I remembered I had put that special dog in my purse that very morning. As I looked for it, I handed her a small mini animal and Bible book and asked where she worked. When I could not locate the small dog, I told her I would get it to her when I found it! As we finished talking, the friend I had arranged to have lunch with arrived and we entered the Restaurant. We enjoyed talking and sharing and having a wonderful meal. I talked with the waitress and then thanked her with a mini animal. As we left our seated area, I met another attendant and talked with him, and gave him a mini animal and Bible promise book as well.

My friend and I parted in the parking lot, and I took time to locate the small dog in my purse, and then brought that to the work site of the woman who had been walking her dog. I was able to leave another mini animal and bible promise book with the receptionist as I handed her the dog for her to give to the woman who had been walking her dog.

The Snake

Once back at my car, I remembered that I had a book that I wanted to give to another waitress at the restaurant we ate at and so I got that from my trunk and brought it back into the restaurant and left it with the Manager to give to that waitress. When I entered, I was able to give a mini animal and bible promise book to the Manager for helping me.

When I returned to my car, I noticed that there was a flattened small dead snake on the pavement right next to my car door.

The dead snake reminded me of the promise that our Lord has overcome evil and that He will rule and reign one day forever, and that made my heart rejoice!

My Trip Home

My trip home included a stop at my family home to help my sister move a plant. Then I went to drop off a promised mini zebra to a woman who loves them along with a bible book. On my way to her home, I noticed a gathering a young people in a parking lot and drove into the parking lot to talk with them. I shared the mini animals and Bible books and invited them to visit Northside Baptist Church.

As I headed for home, I took time to call John H. an old friend from my car phone. My friend told me he had just gotten out of the hospital, and so I prayed for him.

That Night

Once home, I enjoyed a wonderful meal prepared by Audrey with my family. After dinner, Fabien and I watched a taped presentation on how salvation works.

The presenter had a picture of the 'cross' and of a man kneeling before the cross. The word RIGHTEOUSNESS was over the cross and the word SIN was over the man. When the man cried out for forgiveness, the WORDS switched places: RIGHTEOUS now was over the man, and the word SIN was now over the cross. This is a perfect picture of salvation by faith, "not of works lest any man should boast" (Ephesians 2:9).

We are commanded to 'be ready'. Ask the Lord for open doors and opportunities to share your faith! And then take time to get ready! The Lord is faithful to provide us with open doors to bless and encourage one another to have faith. Sometimes it is just a smile, or a few words, but when the door opens, go through and share your testimony whenever you can!

Chapter 12

Be Devoted

Let your heart therefore be wholly devoted to the Lord our God, to walk in His Statutes and to keep His commandments as at this day.

1 Kings 8:61

All In

It's being 'all in' from the time we wake up until the time we go to bed. It's being able to say 'no' to doing things that we might 'like to do' in order to be able to 'do those things that are pleasing in God's sight." It is being willing to 'pick up your cross and follow Him. "Then said Jesus unto his disciples, if any man will come after me, let him deny himself and take up his cross and follow me" (Mathew 16:24).

For those that actually do this, there are unexpected blessings delivered that enable us to continue to move forward.

The Silver Heart

One such unexpected blessing occurred one morning when I woke up. Before I even get out of bed, I say a prayer to the Lord, "Lord, let my eyes be Your eyes, my ears - Your ears, My mouth -Your mouth, My hands - Your hands, my feet – Your feet, my mind – Your mind, my thoughts – Your thoughts: let me be a vessel of honor for Your use today!"

Before I even could open my eyes after my prayer, I suddenly heard a bell ring about 3 times and then within my mind's eye I saw a silver box that had diamonds all around the edge of the box. There was an elaborate pattern within the silver on the top of a silver heart. Then as I looked at that silver box, suddenly a crease appeared in the middle and it opened out from the center, and suddenly smiling faces were coming at me, one after another in rapid succession – those faces were all like real faces, but were in 'black and white' as I saw them. It reminded me of a book having its pages flipped from one to another rapidly. Then one last image appeared and the silver heart box disappeared. My heart was moved by what I had seen. These were all very happy people who came with a smile for me and all appeared to 'know' me, but I did not recognize any of them.

The Lord has promised to fellowship with those who choose to walk with him.

This experience encourages me to encourage you to know beyond a shadow of a doubt that people are being impacted by your walk of faith who you do not currently know, but who will one day be on the other side rejoicing with us and giving praise and glory and honor to the Lord forever and ever for the things He has done for us!

A Reminder

About two years after this had occurred, when I finished giving an animal and Bible promise book to a woman, I looked at her neck, and saw she was wearing a 'silver heart' on a chain that looked a lot like the one I had seen. I asked her about her silver necklace. She told me, "This silver heart is something that was given to me, and I really like it!" I told her, "You are a blessing to me today as well, because of that necklace!"

As I walked away, I thanked the Lord for the opportunity to share His word with her, as well as with those that I meet, and asked him again to not let His word return void to Him!

Chapter 13

God Remembers

Bless the Lord, O my soul, and forget not all His Benefits.

Psalm 103:2

My life includes events, trials, and blessings. One day I received a call from a couple that had rented from me the home that I had used as a rental property. It had been 7 years since I had seen them, but I was delighted to hear from them. I was very happy to hear from them, because they had been amazing renters willing to fix an issue when it occurred. This couple was in VT to visit their daughter and their grandchildren and wanted to stop to visit me. I invited them to come for lunch in our home. The wife was a professional cook and I was able to find one of her recipes on her web site and make it for them.

We enjoyed a wonderful meal together and then we walked around to see the property and the home that they rented from me, which my sister Treya now owns.

As we walked around, the Lord used them to remind me of the many things that had occurred since 2004 when I purchased the property for a home for me and my Dad.

They remembered how things 'used' to be, and they noticed all of the changes that had been made. Their coming to visit highlighted the many 'Blessings' the Lord had bestowed upon me and my sister, Treya.

When they left, we agreed to stay in touch.

Their Surprise

At the time that they ended their renting of the home, they could not get all of their things onto their moving truck. They had left a couple of things behind and had given them to me.

As they got ready to leave the day of their visit, I told them I had something to show them. I then brought them into my living room and showed them one of their rocking chairs that they had gifted to me. The wife exclaimed, "O, that belonged to my husband's grandmother, it was her rocking chair, I cannot believe you still have it!" I replied, "Well, I actually have kept both of the rockers that you gave me, and they are both here waiting for you when you want them back!"

This was truly such a sweet moment for them and for me. A remembrance for me, as well as for them! That our God is able to do abundantly above and beyond all that we can think or ask.

"Now unto him that is able to do exceeding, abundantly above all that we ask or think, according to the power that worketh in us, unto Him be glory in the church by Christ Jesus, throughout all ages, world without end" (Ephesians 3:20).

The Unexpected Connection

One of my assignments was to assist a man whose wife had recently passed. On one of my visits, we decided to go to the grave site where she had been buried. The family had added flowers, around their gravestone and the man wanted to see how things looked. Our visit produced a BIG surprise for both of us!

Once we arrived, we went and sat on a bench in front of the gravestone. We talked about how wonderful the flowers looked planted on either side. The man exclaimed, "What a great job!" Although his faith in the Lord Jesus Christ provided consolation that his wife was with the Lord in heaven, he missed her presence in his life. I told him, "I believe your wife knows we are here. It is our physical bodies that limit our ability to communicate with those who have entered eternity, but we are forever connected within our souls to those we love." As we sat in silence together, I knew he was telling his wife how much he loved and missed her, and I asked the Lord to comfort him.

When he was ready, he stood and I stood and we started to walk away. But I turned and stopped so I could take a picture using my phone of their gravestone with the flowers. Then I pulled up the picture to show the man. As we looked at the phone screen, we were 'surprised' by what we saw. The picture had captured our images making it appear as though we both were inside the stone with her at that very moment. We had left at just the right time, and the picture was taken at just the right angle, for our reflections to appear within the polished stone.

Death is a reminder of the unpredictability of life and of the importance of living one day at a time. When we TRUST in the Lord, He directs our steps and can answer prayer in unexpected ways to provide comfort during times of loss!

Chapter 14

Have A Heart Vision

A new heart also will I give you, and a new spirit will I put within you: and I will take away the stony heart out of your flesh, and I will give you a heart of flesh.

Ezekiel 36:26

One of the great wonders of walking with the Lord's Holy Spirit is being aware of the small miracles that happen in answer to our prayers each day.

One of the most wonderful precious times for me is time set aside in the morning during the week when my two sisters, and our friend Caroline who lives close by are able to visit. We come together before we start our work day to share and to support and help one another as we are able.

During this time, I share a Bible verse, and there is a poetry reading. We then share our thoughts about the wonder of the universe and world that the Lord has created. One morning the poetry reading took on additional significance. The poem was about butterflies. When the mail arrived that same day, there was a special card sent to me from the Pastor's wife who prayed with me, and her card was full of colorful 'butterflies. I took time to write to the Pastor's wife and let her know how blessed I had been by not only her writing to me, but by the card itself. My letter to her said:

Date

Hi Joyce,

Your 'butterfly' card arrived today! This very day, my sisters were reading a morning poem about 'butterflies'. When they finish reading their special poem of inspiration, I shared my own bible reading with them.

Their poem butterfly reading was about how butterflies are cared for and how simple life is for them. My comment to my sisters was, 'We are more valuable than butterflies; the Lord is there to care for us too! We are told to, "Cast all your care upon Him, for He careth for you" (1 Peter 5:7). Other bible verses for today were shared with them as well:

" . . with purpose of heart . . . cleave to the Lord: (Acts 11:23).

"He giveth power to the faint, and to them that have no might" (Isaiah 40:29).

"The Lord knoweth the way" (Psalm 11:6).

"Hide me under the shadow of Thy wings: (Psalm 17:8).

When your card arrived, I took it down to show them. My oldest sister was amazed and said, "This happens to you all the time!"

Then I got to explain that 'salvation is' like a 'marriage commitment" that creates our relationship with God and that has nothing to do with 'religion'. It is truly our asking for 'forgiveness' and acceptance of Jesus's righteousness that 'seals' the contract for each soul and gives the assurance that 'whosoever will may come'. The wonder is that "These things are written that ye may KNOW that ye have eternal life" (1 John 5:13).

Not many Christians realize how very close we are to the return of Jesus in the air for His own. The Lord continues to show me which makes me desire to use every minute that I can to witness, pray and read and study the Bible. These are the things that help us to Praise God, and witness God's goodness and grace.

Divine Provision

The most amazing of all is how the Lord is able to meet our needs not only spiritually, but physically. Prayers were made for Caroline and Adam, after they moved to Vermont from California for them to find a home that would be able to afford. Their search began and one of the homes they were interested in, could not be financed because the home did not have its own well. Other properties were considered, but then that particular home appeared back on a listing at a reduced price, and this time, a well had been drilled for the property. Although they had travelled to help Caroline's Mother, an offer was made by them on the property and the offer was accepted. The financing was approved and efforts began to ensure they could furnish the home at minimal expense. Fabien and I offered our garage as a 'staging area' for storing items for their new home. Both of them came to our home farm and went through items in storage that were 'free' to them from us. Fabien brought his truck and they came with their station wagon. When we left my home farm location, they had a table and chairs, end table, and two rocker chairs, a desk chair, and many other items. After those were loaded onto the truck, we headed back to our home to place them in storage. Fabien commented that the only item they were now missing was a couch. As we came to the end of route 207, Fabien and I noticed that a recliner couch had been brought out and was at the end of a driveway. He pulled over and Caroline and Adam stopped and agreed to go back and look at the couch. The couch would work. We went an emptied the truck and Adam and Fabien went back to get that couch. When they finally moved in, Fabien and I were amazed at how each room had furniture that fit perfectly within the space. The extra chairs needed for their table, and other items were provided by other members of our family to them. There would be no way of knowing for anyone visiting the 'miracle' of the Lord actually providing the furnishings for them for their new home, at relatively little to no cost.

The White Horse

Last night when Fabien was watching a western, when I walked by him, he said, "Look Dawn – there is a WHITE horse!" I looked to see a beautiful 'white' horse running very fast on the screen. I told Jesus quietly in my heart, 'Lord, you are coming on a white horse! You are faithful and True' (Rev. 19:11). I continued to look at that white horse as it ran very fast and I told Jesus, "I am so happy you are coming!" Then I kissed Fabien and told him I was going to bed. On my bed stand there were three bible audio programs that have the entire bible recorded in audio. I decided to use the Bible recorder that was in the middle. Each recorder is set at different parts of the bible. When I turned that recorder on to listen before I went to sleep. That recorder began at: "To him that overcometh I will grant to sit with me in my throne" (Rev. 3:21). And Chapter 4 in Revelation gave the account of the four horses and of a 'white horse' that will begin the 'time of Jacob's trouble, a time of great distress on earth. My commitment to the Lord began when I was 23, a very sincere real commitment. I have tried to serve Jesus since I gave my life to Him. Life is not easy! Challenges come when we least expect them and when we are not prepared to deal with them. I believe this happens to enable us to 'give God glory'. When we know that we need Him, we pray the most! When we witness His faithfulness to provide a way of escape through hard times, our faith is solidified and strengthened!

Chapter 15

Be Joyful

I say unto you, that likewise joy shall be in heaven, over one

sinner that repenteth.

(Jesus)

John 15:7

The focus of our world has nothing to do with the focus of heaven. Before one can 'repent' one must be aware that they are in need of 'repentance'. Believers who have acknowledged belief in who Jesus Christ is, and was, and will be; who have recognized the fact that not any one of us is 'good enough' to enter the perfection of heaven, are the ones that have the opportunity to 'ask' the Lord for forgiveness, and receive eternal life. Jesus referred to this as being 'born again'. This brings a joy that passes all understanding, and opens a door for unexpected delights from the Lord.

The Picture

When I had finished helping our new friend with her move, I had made a commitment to give things away. I did this because I know that "life does not consist of the abundance of the things that we possess' (Luke 12:15), I was determined to sort through and give away as much as possible from our home and garage. My effort would include asking my husband Fabien about things he owned and whether they could be given away. One of the things that he approved for taking to Habitat was a drawing of a picture of himself sitting on the tractor. He had gotten the picture as a gift several years before from a friend. His head within that picture was very large, and the tractor he was sitting on was very small. It was a wonderful caricature image and it looked just like him, but what to do with it!?   So, into the load of my car it went to go to Habitat.

Three years later

Our family grew to include 6-7 people and when we would meet to eat together during the week, we were short chairs. When one of my sister's announced, "Habitat is having a one-day sale that is 40% off!", I told Fabien, "We need to go and look for 2 chairs that will match our table so we aren't having to pull chairs from other rooms to host dinner." He agreed and off we went. There were two Habitat stores in the next town, one being merged into a new location. We went to their new location. Once there, we walked around.

We found chairs, some were too small, others too large, and some not strong enough, so we left with nothing. As we travelled home, I said, "Let's go to the original location and see if they have anything there!" Fabien replied, "I don't even think it is open, but we can go check."

When we arrived, it was open, and we found a chair that was strong enough and the right size for our table. Both of us were happy to have found at least one chair that would work. As we pulled the chair out of the small corner that we had found it in, we found something else.

Yes, there was the picture of Fabien sitting on the tractor! He exclaimed, "There's my picture!" I said, 'Indeed! Don't you remember your telling me to go ahead and take it here?!" He said, "Yes, but It is disheartening that no one has purchased it!" Then he added, "I'm taking it back! I'm not leaving myself here to be 'thrown away'!"

Off we went to the checkout with our chair and the picture. Even though we had given the picture to Habitat, we would need to purchase it back!

As I handed the picture to the clerk, I said, "We came here for this chair, but when we spotted this picture, we had to get it because it looks just like my husband."

She looked at the picture and looked at Fabien standing behind me, and exclaimed, "That's amazing! Yes, it DOES look JUST like him!" I replied, "Well, it LOOKS just like him, because it IS him!" She exclaimed, "No!" I replied, "Yes, we brought the picture here 3 years ago, and no one purchased it, so we are taking it home!"

One of the other clerks actually was related to my husband, and she came to see what was going on. When she saw what was happening, she laughed, "So no one wanted you!" Fabien replied, "I guess not!" We all laughed.

When we got home, Fabien said, "I'm going to keep this in my shop, above my work bench, I have just the place for it!" We both were amazed that we had located something we had given away, and had 'redeemed it' back to where it could be appreciated.

We are like that picture. Many of us feel that we have no place, and no real value in this world. When we compare ourselves with others, we can feel like we are not smart enough, not pretty enough, or handsome enough, not talented enough, not rich enough, etc. But the Lord made each of us and tells us that, 'the redemption of our soul is precious' (Psalm 49:8). So precious that the Lord sent his only begotten son, Jesus to die so that we could be purchased back!

When we are out of the fold of God, we do not know our true value. Like the picture, we only realize our real value when we are found by the Lord. We are valued and loved, and have been purchased back; and there is joy in heaven when a person comes to the Lord.

"Likewise, joy shall be in heaven over one sinner that repenteth." (Luke 15: 7)

Chapter 16

Believe His Promises

And whatsoever ye shall ask in my name, that will I do, that the Father may be glorified in the Son. If ye shall ask any thing in my name, I will do *It*. If ye love me, keep my commandments.
John 14: 13-15

God's promises are real. God is able to do abundantly above all we can ask or think (Ephesians 3:20). There are some prayers that are answered immediately, others take a few days, some weeks, some months, some years. The most amazing part of prayer is that the Lord is so FAITHFUL! It would take over 50 years for the Lord to answer one of my prayers.

The Prayer

When I was a teenager I met and dated a man who had a brother. I met his brother G. when he returned from being in the service. The brother G. met a beautiful woman named M. and me and M. became best friends. The brother G. married that woman and she had three children, all boys. I was asked to be the 'God- Mother" for their first son P. for which I readily agreed. It had been my plan to marry the man I was dating, but my life would not go in that direction. When that relationship ended and we went different ways, my ability to visit that entire family became blocked. I was asked to not stay in touch at all, and I honored that request.

Years passed, and I thought often of the oldest boy P. and of the other two boys as well.

A few years later, I accepted Jesus and invited His Holy Spirit to come and live within my heart and began my very first prayer list. My friend M. and her husband G. and the boys were on my prayer list. My prayer was for their protection and for the Lord to make them aware of His great love for each of them.

It would be many years before I would meet M. again. I had stopped at a hardware store and as I turned around an aisle, there was my best friend M. We visited and chatted about our lives. She told me her sons were all grown up, had sons of their own and she told me she had been battling a disease.

More years past when I learned she had passed. Her husband passed as well, a few years later. And now their three sons were really on my mind.

50 Years later

One day I prayed very hard that the Lord would intervene in the lives of M. and G.'s three sons, I asked the Lord to send someone to tell them about the Love of the Lord for them. I told the Lord, "Perhaps even I might be the one to share that information with them! But how would I ever be able to connect with them? You would have to be the one who would make that happen, because I cannot just show up at their house unannounced!"

My life experience of serving the Lord gave me peace, because I know the Lord answers prayer and I praised him for sending someone, even if it was not me.

Rehab Visits

My husband Fabien and I purchased a stove pipe for his son's home from a man who was rebuilding his family home from scratch by himself. As I shared my mini animal and bible book with the man who sold us the stove pipe, he explained that his Dad had passed and his Mom was in a home. I asked where the home was and learned that the Rehab Home was next to where we lived. I told him, "I would like to stop and meet your Mom!" He replied, "I am sure she would enjoy a visitor."

The next time I was in town, I stopped and introduced myself to the man's mother and brought her some fresh blueberries. She invited me to stop anytime.

Then I learned that one of my friends Tami had a mother in the very same Rehab Center! I told Tami that I was visiting someone in that Rehab, and asked if it would be okay for me to stop and visit her Mom. Tami agreed.

The next time I visited both Mom's and brought them scrap books of pictures of birds and butterflies that my friend Karey had made for older people she was assigned to help.

One of the joys of my visits, was to bring fresh fruit, and treats that they loved. One day, as I was leaving, I met a woman on my way out and gave her encouragement with one of my mini animals and Bible book. As she took them, she said, "I am here to see my husband. I can only come once a week because I live a long distance away." I replied, "I stop here quite often to visit two of my friend's mothers." She replied, "When you visit them, please visit my husband as well and pray with him! I am sure your visit would cheer him up!" She gave me his name, and I promised I would stop and visit with him as well.

On my next visit, after seeing both of my two regular mothers, I asked the nurse at the desk for the room of the man I had promised to visit. I easily found the room. As I entered the room, I asked the man in the first section of the room if he was this man. He replied, "No, he is in the next bed." I went around the pulled curtain and introduced myself, I said, "Your wife asked me to stop and pray with you." The man thanked me for coming. We visited and before I left, I asked him, "Would you like me to pray, before I leave?" He replied, "Yes! I would!" We held hands and I prayed for him. When I asked if he would like me to stop again, he said 'Yes!'

As I left the room, I had to go past the first man again. I stopped to ask that man, "What is your name?" He replied, "P." Rarely do I ask for a last name, but I felt compelled to ask him for his last name. He replied, "P.G." I then spelled the last name back to him that he had spoken to me. He corrected me and respelled his last name. I stood almost in shock. I was talking to my best girlfriend's M.'s son, the very son that I was the God-Mother of from so many years ago! I said, "I believe I know your Mom and Dad; your Mom is M.?" He replied, 'Yes!" I said, "And your Dad is G." He replied, "Yes!" I said, "I was best friends with your Mother! I remember the very last time I saw you. Your mom was pulling you in a wagon down a dirt road when you were very young." He looked back at me perplexed. I added, "You have two brothers as well." He replied, "Yes!". I said, "Well, I have been praying for you and your two brothers now for many, many years - and here you are right now in front of me!"

I said, "You are talking to your God Mother." We both just looked at each other for a long time. It was just unbelievable! I smiled at him, "You look just like your Mom and your Dad!" I explained how my life had gone in a different direction, and how I had not married the man who was his Dad's brother. I explained that I had been asked to not contact the family as it was too difficult for them and for me. He married someone who would give him children, which I could not do. I asked, "How old are you?" He replied, "Fifty-one!" Tears were in my eyes. as I told him I had been praying for him for over 50 years. I asked, "What happened to you?" He replied, "I had a stroke when I was helping one of my brothers and I fell and broke a leg, and I did get better from that, but then I had another stroke and ended up in another home in another town. Then last week I had another stroke, and they moved me to this Home just two days ago." I looked at him in complete amazement.

Two weeks ago, I had prayed very hard that the Lord would send someone to these three boys that I had known so long ago. I told the Lord, "I do not want to get on the other side and meet M. and G. and not be able to rejoice with them on how you, Lord, can answer prayers." I added, "I would love to be the person who gets to talk with them but I cannot just go and look them up and appear at their door! You, Lord, would have to arrange for me to meet them. And the one I really would like to see again is P.G. because he is my God child!"

Now, here I was standing right in front of P.G.! And I was here because of my meeting that woman on my way out, two weeks before, at the exit of the home who asked me to stop and see her husband who was in the very room that P.G. was assigned to after he had a stroke. The fact that he had been moved from a Home in another town into the very Rehab Home that I was visiting, was truly an answered prayer!

We continued to talk. I left him a Bible promise book and an eagle and asked him if he would be willing to read the little book. He replied, "Yes, I will look at it for sure!" I said, "And would it be okay with you if I come to visit you again?" He said, "Well, I will be here for sure, and yes, feel free to stop and visit me next time you come." I replied, "I will stop by when I am here to see you and will bring you something when I come."

Even now as I write this, I cannot help but smile, and want to cry at the same time. The man that is my 'God child' I now get to visit and help at the very time when he needs the help the most! I can see Jesus, M. and G. smiling in heaven! Can't you!? And the Lord arranged for me to actually be the one to share my faith in God with P. for whom I was God Mother.

A Lovely Surprise

Valentine's Day is one day that I like to be able to do something special for Fabien. My prayer was to the Lord for something that would be unusual, yet meaningful, and that would cost little to nothing. My goal was to convey my appreciation to him and for his presence in my life.

Knowing meals mean a lot to him, I decided to make him deviled eggs. I boiled up a dozen of them. As I cut them in half to remove the center yolks, I was amazed with what one of those eggs had inside. As I opened it up, I looked and there in front of me was a perfectly forms 'heart' shaped yolk, on both sides. One of the sides actually had the white of the egg that was formed into a 'heart' shape as well. I had to stand there and look at this sight again and again, to convince myself that what I was actually seeing was 'real'. This egg yolk would not be removed. It would remain as it was so that when I gave Fabien his plate of food, I could place the special 'heart' egg on his plate. I told him, "And here is something extra special for your for-Valentine's Day!" As he looked at the heart shaped yoke inside the egg, he exclaimed, "Well, that must have been a really happy chicken to lay such a 'Lovely Egg"!"

"Yes, indeed!", I replied! We both laughed and I took time to take a picture of the heart shaped egg so I could share the wonder of the Lord's ability to answer a unique prayer in a very special way!

"Now unto him that is able to do exceedingly abundantly above all that we ask o think according to the power that worketh in us, unto him be glory in the church by Christ Jesus throughout all ages, world without end. Amen" (Ephesians 3:20-21).

Delight thyself also in the LORD: and he shall give thee the desires of **thine** heart" (Psalm 37:4).

We truly shortchange ourselves from experiencing the 'smiles' that come from heaven when we are NOT willing to walk in obedience to the leading of God's Holy Spirit. When we are willing to be the Lord's hands, feet, ears, eyes, and mouth – God meets us in amazingly wonderful ways.

Chapter 17

Be Sure to Laugh

A merry heart doeth good like a medicine: But a broken spirit drieth the bones.

Proverbs 17:22

We are instructed by the Lord to 'not lean unto our own understanding' for a very good reason. When we determine to assess our lives based upon only what we can 'understand' during our moments of crisis or trial, we rob ourselves of having 'peace' in the midst of the storm. The greatest gift the Lord gives us is His ability to give us His peace when we bring our concerns to the Lord in prayer. This is a peace that surpasses our ability to understand. The Bible is full of accounts of how God did 'work things together for good'.

The Call

My own realization of how limited human reasoning came as the result of a phone call. My only brother had been doing his job, and realized there was a kitten that needed help. The mother cat had a 'litter' of many kittens, but this one was the smallest one – the 'runt' of her litter. He had called and asked us to help with this kitten. My sister Audrey had rescued a feral female cat who had 11 kittens; and her milk supply was not enough to feed all the little hungry mouths seeking milk every few hours. Audrey had taken them and fed those kittens with a small bottle until they were weaned and able to be given away.

My brother's heart of compassion caused him to scoop up the 'runt' and take it home. He was determined to feed and care for it by himself, but it took just one day for him to realize he needed help. His work hours were too long for him to be able to feed this kitten every few hours, as well as clean and care for it. His call for help ended up with my role which was to simply go and pick up the kitten from his home and bring it to Audrey, who lives on the lower level of my home.

Once I arrived at my brother's home, I located the kitten who was on the floor under a blanket next to a 'cooking pot' equipped with a blanket that had been made into its bed. The kitten had somehow been able to climb out of that deep pot. When I picked up the kitten, its little claws pulled the blanket up as I lifted. I carefully detached its claws from the blanket, and could feel that the kitten's paws were cold. I held the kitten in my hands to warm it up and attempted to give it a bottle of milk I had found on the counter, but the kitten would not eat. I placed the kitten inside my jacket, and grabbed the pot and the milk and headed out the door. During the entire car trip home, the kitten continued to object very loudly with 'kitten chatter'. I 'talked' to it, and 'sang' to it, but this kitten was not happy! When I finally got to Audrey's, I picked up the 'cooking pot' on the passenger seat, and brought both inside. Audrey quickly stopped everything she was doing. I handed her the kitten, and she held it and talked to it as she heated up a small bottle and gave it the heated milk. She too noticed the kitten's feet were cold. Audrey then placed the kitten on a heating pad and covered it up to allow it to sleep. This kitten's journey continued with lots of verbal objections.

Audrey quickly determined that the kitten needed a bath. The smell of the barn and its own lack of mother cat care, made it smell pretty bad. The kitten didn't like the warm bath, but that bath removed the fleas that

were on it. As she dried it off with a soft cloth, the volume of noise coming out of that kitten hit a new peak volume.
Listening to the 'racket' one would believe the kitten was being 'destroyed' rather than 'delivered'.

I thought about how little that kitten knew. I remembered some of my own life situations which now flashed in my memory. Suddenly, I laughed! Here was a perfect example of how the Lord comes to us and picks us up and 'delivers' us, just as this kitten was delivered.

We are very much like the kitten! We immediately object! We, too, are very vocal. We are sure we are being slain and that the whole situation is just dreadful. We want to be out of it as quickly as possible. We truly believe, like the kitten, that the more we object, the more likely it is that the situation will change. And amazingly the situation does change, but not due to any of our objections!

Like the kitten, we have a very limited perspective of everything that is happening in our lives. The great news is that we have the opportunity to equip ourselves with God's promises that are contained within the Bible. These promises are from God to us, specifically for the trials that are sure to come our way.

The First of Nine Lives

Audrey named the kitten Grady because he was into everything like an equipment grader! His curiosity that almost killed the 'cat' moment came when Audrey was working in her kitchen and he was scurrying about. She opened the lower freezer door of the fridge to get something. When she went back to doing things, she noticed that Grady was missing. She looked around and realized the last time she saw him was when she was at the refrigerator door, and when she had the freezer door open. Impulsively she opened the freezer door to see. Yes, there was Grady looking back at her. He was bewildered and felt a little cold, but he had not been in the freezer very long. When I told Fabien what happened, he exclaimed, "We almost hat a 'cat-sicle", and that is why they say, "Curiosity Killed the Cat!"

Our own curiosity causes us too, like Grady, be into the lures of this temporary world seeking to find something new. Fortunately, the Lord, like Audrey, can come and find us and get us back on track.

"Wait on the Lord, be of good courage, and He shall strengthen thine heart: Wait I say on the Lord" (Psalm 27:14).

This Christian song entitled, 'When we See Christ" sums it all up:

'Often times the day seems long, our trials hard to bear,
We're tempted to complain, to murmur and despair,
But Christ will soon appear, to catch His Bride away,
All tears forever over, in God's eternal day:
It will be worth it all, when we see Jesus,
Life's trials will seem so small, when we see Christ.
One glimpse of his dear face, all sorrow will erase
So bravely run the race, till we see Christ.'

Chapter 18

Be of Service
Truly, I tell you a servant is not greater than His Master.
(Jesus)

John 13:16

Being a 'servant' means you have a "Master". Jesus made it very clear that no one could serve 'two' masters. There is an immediate conflict when our hearts are 'divided'. True discipleship produces within our heart a deep desire to 'align' and be 'obedient to' the Lord Jesus Christ and the leading of His Holy Spirit. This desire is a result of knowing the price that was paid for our redemption. We have total forgiveness and assurance of being an 'heir' of 'eternal life'. Eternal life begins right now, as the 'life' of God that is within us is allowed to direct our steps each day.

When we consecrate our lives to God, He begins to sanctify us unto Himself. Jesus is our example. The gospel of Mark contains Jesus's life as a 'servant'. Jesus was driven into the wilderness after He was baptized by John the Baptist, for even He needed to be tried in the fire of life's temptations. There he remained for 40 days and 40 nights. At the end of that trial, when he was the weakest, he experienced a full assault by the prince of this world, Lucifer. The question was, would Jesus allow God to meet his needs, or would he resort to meeting his own needs with the gifts God had given him? Jesus passed the test using God's Word 'man shall not live by 'bread' alone but by every word that proceedeth out of the mouth of God' (Matthew 4:4). Then angels came to Him.

Upon His return, he continued in prayer and fasting and the Holy Spirit of God remained upon Him. Jesus was an early riser, and went alone in the morning to pray, and then He was out doing His Father's will. His disciples followed him day after day. Each day was full of activity and service wherever they went, serving others all along the way. Make no mistake, Jesus knew the Old Testament thoroughly and quoted it often. He amazed everyone that heard Him with His ability to understand and apply the prophecy's contained in the Old Testament with authority and power. Jesus was Prophet, Priest and King.

Old Testament

The accounts in the Old Testament affirm the power of God to work in amazing ways to meet our needs during very trying times. One such account reveals how God used divine intervention to arrange circumstances to fulfill His purpose.

Gehiza was a servant of Elisha (a type of Christ) who witnessed the raising of a boy to life by his master Elisha and the return of that boy alive to its mother. The healing was accompanied by a warning to the mother to flee with the boy to another land because there would be a severe famine in the land for seven years. The mother listened and left her home with her son.

Seven years past. Then Gehiza was called by the King and asked to tell the account of what happened to this woman. At the very same time that Gehiza gave his account, the woman and her son (who had travelled back to the land to reclaim their home and land) entered the King's palace. As Gehiza spoke, the woman interrupted him and pleaded with the King for her land. Gehazi said, 'My Lord, O King, **this is** the woman and this is her son whom Elisha restored to life" (11 Kings 8:1-6). God had arranged the perfect timing for the King to bring Gehiza to the Palace to give his account and simultaneously for the woman and her son who received the miracle, to come to the King to request her land - both occurred at the exact same time, after seven years!

Gehiza and this woman and the King experienced God's priceless, precious promises. God continues to work in these same ways, even now for each of us!

The reason we are not aware of these miraculous connections is due to our lack of commitment, consecration, and sanctification. The more of the 'world' we have in 'us' the less power the Lord has over us. In effect, we have 'two' masters. We claim to belong to the Lord, but many times the claim is in 'word' only. Our hearts are still 'connected' too much to the 'things of this world' and it is those very 'things' that divert our attention and our time and blind us to spiritual things. This world is full of 'very good' things, but when we are about those 'very good things' we miss out on God's best. What each of us is truly hungry for is the 'perfect will of God' for us. That is where the 'joy *in* the Lord' dwells fully.

When you make a decision to be '*all in*' -available, ready and willing to be a 'servant', the Lord will bring you closer and closer. The road you travel will become 'less travelled', and narrower, until the path becomes like a single line. God *will* give us the desires of our heart, when **He alone** is our pure delight! God delights in answering our prayers. God is waiting and wanting each of 'us' to *come closer*. A 'snuggle up' kind of closeness with Him.

God has answered my prayers and some answers have brought tears of gratitude to my eyes; my trials also have brought tears of sorrow. The overwhelming wonder of it all, is that those very trials have been worked together for my good, and produced within me a greater willingness to yield to God's guidance. The closeness that I have desired, I have struggled to attain, but through fasting, prayer and praising it is available to whoever choses to walk the narrow path.

The two things that we lack in our world are truly tied together: Joy and workers.

The **joy** of experiencing God's promises is available for all, for indeed God's harvest is plentiful. The **'laborers'** are indeed few. Therefore, let us honor the request of Jesus who asked us to pray this prayer: "Pray ye therefore the Lord of the harvest, that He would send forth laborers into His harvest (Matthew 9:38).

People who are 'in love' with the Lord and who desire a relationship with Him *over* **everything else** will experience God's Priceless, Precious Promises!

"And ye shall seek me and find me when ye shall search for me with all your heart" (Jeremiah 29:13).

The Dream

I had a dream that I went to a cottage to think and be alone with the Lord. Once at the cottage, two pastors spoke and delivered good messages. After the messages, the television was on for people to watch programs. When I requested that it be turned off, the two pastors refused to turn it off. I explained to both pastors that their messages were good but that was not enough for them or for us. We needed 'separation' from the world's way of thinking. I explained to them that without being separate, we **all** miss out, in our ability to be of real service to the Lord Jesus Christ. As they appeared perplexed, I woke up, realizing the importance of 'separation'.

Thy word have I hid in my heart that I might not sin against thee. Psalm 119:11

And take the helmet of salvation and the sword of the spirit which is the word of God. Ephesians 6:17

Let the word of Christ dwell in you richly in all wisdom, teaching and admonishing one another in psalms and hymns and spiritual songs singing with grace in your hearts to the Lord. Colossians 3:16

One Body

We are to be 'one' body, and like our physical body that has many parts, we are to work together using the abilities we have to serve each other and those we love. Those in ministry, or who teach, must wait on the

Lord's leading for messages. And just as our body needs our care to be healthy, our spiritual soul needs attention and care. It is by reading the Bible that we gain an understanding of how we need to live our lives. Read Romans 12. There we are instructed to abhor evil and to cleave to what is good, to be kind to one another, to be willing to get involved and to serve. We are NOT promised a life without trials, but are told to patiently wait and pray when we are asked to go through them. We are instructed to be instant in prayer, to give of what we have, and to bless those who are critical of what we do. Our service is to be true, not speaking harshly to one another, or returning a rude remark when we have received one. Rather, as much as possible, we are to live at peace with and not make room within us for anger.

When we do these things, we will not be overcome with evil, but we overcome evil with good!

Like in my dream, none of us are to be high minded or to think we are better than any one else, or that any one is better than us. Opportunities abound around us for us to touch each other with words of kindness, love and encouragement. Our 'hour glass' of opportunities for service will come to and end for each of us on earth, when time for us will be 'no more'.

"Soon our pilgrimage will cease." Robert Lowry 1828-1899

"Face to face I shall see Him by and by." Carrie Breck 1855-1934

What can possibly encourage us to be consistently about our Father's business? What can we do, to help us not be blind to truth? It begins with a choice to be like Jesus and to daily read the Bible for ourselves. The Bible assures us that the spiritual world of Love and Truth will rule in the end. When we understand that, we will be motivated to choose to live each day with that in mind. Each of us will leave our physical body, to enter 'eternal life.'

"Living always in the sight of God we are more studious to please Him."
Thomas Manton

Chapter 19

Have One Purpose Only

Abide in me, and I in you.
As the branch cannot bear fruit of itself, except it abide on the vine;
no more can ye, except ye abide in me.

John 15:4

Walking with God's Holy Spirit's leading is a bit like being an ice skater. There is a lot of preparation required before a professional skater even puts on their skates. We as Christians are expected to prepare ourselves each morning for His service. What does that look like? It means rising early to provide time to just sit and read the Bible. It means having a Journal ready to take notes to remember what verses are making an impression on your heart. It means starting the day with 'prayer' for the things you are required to accomplish, and for those things that will just 'show up' that you are unaware of coming your way! It means praying for those you love, who are on your mind. It means having a 'prayer list' to jog your memory so you can continue to keep those in prayer who are experiencing trials and hardships. It means taking time to thank and praise the Lord for hearing your prayers and asking Him to help you to hear his slightest whisper and to commit yourself to walk the path that the Lord has prepared for you. It means being committed to allow His Holy Spirit to guide and direct your thoughts.

"My heart is fixed on God, let me sing and give praise to thee. Be thou exalted O God above the heavens" (Psalm 15:57).

The Lord knows our very thoughts. "Thou O God has heard my vows, give me the heritage of those that fear Thy name" (Psalm 61:5).

Walking with the Lord is like being on skates for the first time. It is not a pretty sight! There is a lot of unsteadiness when you first stand up! And moving forward without falling flat on your rear is just not possible! There is a lot of hesitation, many wrong turns, and much relief when the day is done and the 'skates' come off!

But over time, this balancing act of 'Abiding' within the presence of the Lord, becomes a 'joy' filled with expectation and delight. The power of God's Spirit can move us just like being on skates, with a flow and synergy that is not possible apart from His Holy Spirit. When we are successful with giving our testimony to another person, it as if we have taken a great leap into the air and done a complete circle before landing on our feet again. There have been days when the Lord has taken me for quite a ride! The more we 'abide' the greater the 'current' reward of His presence.

Think of an ice skater who is able to skate with a partner. They move side by side, in complete harmony, one guiding the other through a routine, holding a hand, allowing one to 'spin' apparently effortlessly around and around, and then coming back together again.

My days are a lot like that. Some days I groan and struggle to get up, some days I struggle to 'stay' up and not go back to bed. Some days I wonder if the Lord will even speak to me, and some days I am so tired, I wonder if I will even 'get it' if the Lord *does* speak to me. But without fail, when I put in the effort, the Lord ALWAYS shows up! And those days are truly blessed with His presence, and His leading, step by step, to do the next thing at hand, and the next, and the next, and the next. Then finally the day is over, and I get to reflect and ponder all the wonderful moments that we have shared together. Whether it involved making the bed, or doing the laundry, or cleaning the bathroom, getting the mail, writing a letter, etc. etc., etc. Each day I pack my purse and my pockets with Bible tracts and books, and with my mini-animals and ask the Lord to help me to 'see' the opportunities, and to prepare the hearts of those that I meet to be open to receiving His Word. I pray the Lord will help me to know what to say, and how to say it. I ask that my words be more than 'words' that those I meet may feel the love that the Lord has for them! The times when I am blessed with meeting someone is like being able to do a jump! Service to the Lord requires us to be yielded. We are following the steps of the Master. We are required to 'begin again' and 'again' and again. To accomplish what is difficult, we will fall down, and have to get back up and try again. Like the ice skaters, we are working at it, and even that work is pleasing in the Lord's sight.

In ice skating there are jumps: the salchow, toe loop, loop, flip, Lutz, and axel. Some named by the skaters (Salchow, Lutz and Axel) who invented them. My most challenging spiritual jumps are when I encounter someone who tells me they are a Buddhist or an Atheist, or an Agnostic. My first encounters with each were miserable failures. Not only would they not accept my Bible books, but I was like a deer in the headlights not knowing what to say to them. It has taken time for me to pray and find my balance.

To the Buddhist I can say, 'Your belief in Karma and reincarnation are noble. I encourage you to learn about Jesus Christ. Jesus is the only one that has risen from the dead."

To the Atheist I can now say, "I respect you because "FAITH is the substance of things hoped for, the evidence of things not seen."

To the Agnostic, I can now say, "I know you do not feel there is enough evidence to have faith, but my own experience gives me hope for what cannot be seen, and I believe Jesus Christ came and died and rose again, and has promised eternal life to all who come to Him."

When I encounter someone who tells me they are 'all set', I ask them if there is anyone in their life that is hurting or suffering, that perhaps the Lord wants them to provide a poem of comfort to them in their time of need, someone who I will never meet, but these Bible books they can share with them. Most of the time, they accept and say, "Thank you."

When I encounter someone who refuses to take anything that I have to offer, I quickly ask them to forgive me for interrupting their day. I tell them my intent was not to be a problem, but to be a blessing and then I thank them for their kindness in taking time to even listen to me.

I believe these encounters are like those ice skaters who travel around on the ice, getting ready to throw themselves up into the air, trusting they will land on their feet! Take time to watch a pair of winning ice-skating couples on U-Tube. There is joy and wonder on their faces when they finish a routine. They know they have done their very best and they have been successful! Then they have tears of joy – those are the kind of tears I want in my life!

Perfect Timing

What creates excellence is 'perfect timing'. Timing is involved with everything on earth. Solomon wrote 'to everything there is a season and a time for every purpose under heaven' (Ecclesiastes 3:1). Plants require time to grow and mature, just as humans. Spiritual growth is the same.

What is of great comfort is that there is actually a purpose behind when we are asked to 'wait'. One of the hardest things to do is to wait, but waiting is what produces spiritual growth. We are instructed, "add to your faith virtue, and to virtue knowledge, and to knowledge temperance, and to temperance patience and to patience godliness, and to godliness brotherly kindness and to brotherly kindness, charity" (2 Peter 1:5-7)

So, waiting is not 'wasted time.' Waiting is actually an exercise of faith in the goodness of God who has promised to work all for our good. It is during times when we must wait that the Lord is able to fill those moments with His assurance of His presence in the midst of our trials.

Knowing that God is with me even in the midst of a trial is one of His greatest treasures.

So, Lord, provide us with the faith we need to 'believe' and to be willing to 'wait' upon you for your will to be done in and through us. To 'trust' that you are indeed in control, and to wait for your perfect timing.

"Wait on the Lord, be of good courage and he shall strengthen thy heart, wait, I say, on the Lord" (Psalm 27:14).

And as we wait, we are told to offer praises to God, especially in the midst of a trial, for this is a sweet 'smelling' sacrifice to the Lord.

"By Him therefore, let us offer the sacrifice of praise to God continually; that is, the fruit of our lips giving thanks to His name. But to do good and to communicate forget not: for with such sacrifices God is well pleased" (Hebrews 13:15-16).

"Seek not happiness apart from holiness; nor rest apart from Jesus, nor pleasure apart from pleasing God." Charles Surgeon – Flowers p. 235

Chapter 20

Celebrate Each Day

Yea, though I walk through the valley of the shadow of death, I will fear no evil: for thou art with me; thy rod and thy staff they comfort me.

Psalm 23:4

Jesus lived to be 33 years old. His ministry started at age 30 and lasted just 3 years. Matthew, Mark, Luke and John contain the accounts of all that happened day by day, month by month, year by year. The twelve apostles became His disciples. Every parable that Jesus told, was explained to them later when they were alone with Him. The accounts tell us that Jesus viewed a work day as being 12 hours, not our typical 8 hours of work during a day. "Are there not twelve hours in a day?" (John 11:9). The Jewish nation considered a day 12 hours and a night 12 hours. The group was so busy doing the things at hand with the Lord, that at the end of each day they were exhausted, yet very aware of the joy of being in the presence of the Son of Man, who was the Savior sent by God to redeem us. After Jesus was resurrected and appeared to the disciples he said, "Why are ye troubled: and why do thoughts arise in your hearts? Behold my hands and my feet, that it is I myself; handle me, and see, for a spirit hath not flesh and bones, as ye see me have." (Luke 24:38-39) Jesus even asked that they give him 'meat' to prove that he was human! Then he proclaimed, "These are the words which I spoke unto you, while I was yet with you, that all things must be fulfilled which were written in the law of Moses, and in the prophets, and in the psalms concerning me" (Luke 24"44).

We are no different than the early disciples of Jesus Christ. When we consecrate our time and talents to the Lord, He will keep us and guide us in those things that bring Him glory.

Often times we will be like Peter asking questions, and lacking understanding. The presence of God's Holy Spirit is the same today as it was after Jesus sent it upon the disciples.

"For we are His workmanship, created in Christ Jesus unto good works, which God hath before ordained that we should walk in them" (Ephesians 2:10).

The truth is each of us has a certain number of days that we will live on earth. When we are young it seems like we have all the time in the world. When we are older, we realize how very fast the days pass. There is coming a day when we will be asked to give an account to the Lord of what we have done during our days on earth.

It is my belief that everything will be turned upside down when we enter eternity. The value of our choices will be viewed differently because they are not to be based upon human understanding. What will be rewarded in heaven will be the choices we made that brought us into contact with others, the service we were able to give to others, those non-monetary things we accomplished. And, 'how' we did things will matter! "Whatsoever ye do, do it heartily unto the Lord and not unto men;

knowing that of the Lord ye shall receive the reward of the inheritance: for ye serve the Lord Christ" (Colossians 3:23-24)

Some days we will feel like Stephen, when we share our faith in Jesus and people are not only not interested in what we have to say, but who are ready to condemn and stone us!

And like Stephen, we will have the chance to declare, "Lay not this sin to their charge" (Acts 7:60).

Jesus delivered the Sermon on the Mount to encourage those who choose to follow to not be easily offended, but to pray for those who persecute us. "Blessed are ye, when men shall revile you, and persecute you, and shall say all manner of evil against you falsely, for my sake. Rejoice, and be exceeding glad: for great is your reward in heaven: for so persecuted they the prophets which were before you" (Matthew 5:11-12).

Jesus had his last words on the cross, "Father forgive them for they know not what they do" (Luke 23:24).

His teachings ask us to be like him. "Love your enemies, bless them that curse you, do good to them that hate you, and pray for them which despitefully use you, and persecute you; that he may be the children of your Father which is in heaven: for He maketh His sun to rise on the evil and on the good, and sendeth rain on the just and on the unjust" (Matthew 5:45).

The day is coming when Jesus Christ will rule and reign forever. We are told to comfort one another. "For the Lord himself shall descend from heaven with a shout, with the voice of the archangel, and with the trump of God; and the dead in Christ shall rise first, then we which are alive and remain shall be caught up together with them in the clouds, to meet the Lord in the air, and so shall we ever be with the Lord. Wherefore comfort one another with these words" (1 Thessalonians 4:16-18).

When we work to make the most of each day, we are less prone to put off doing things until tomorrow. And **one day**, when we will find ourselves, rather unexpectedly in His Presence – to **Celebrate** - forever!

Chapter 21

Live for God

His ways are everlasting.

Habakkuk 3:6

The Lord has told us to "come to Him' for a reason. Life is extremely complex, and when we attempt to manage its details without divine assistance, we make a very bad choice. To the exhausted, worn out stressed and heavy laden with burdens crowd, Jesus declares that 'His burden is light'. When we decide to make the Lord our top priority, we align with truth and His Holy Spirit, and that allows His very presence to abide in us, and work through us. A place where, in spite of how busy the day, the Lord makes it become manageable 'moments' of activity. When life is lived this way, there is spiritual rest in the midst of chaos and storms, because we are able to quickly 'connect' to the power of God's Holy Spirit and that allows Him to answer our prayers in non-understandable ways. Sometimes the Lord has sent a person to assist me, or had people be right where they needed to be when I arrived. This produces such an awareness of His majesty that my heart MUST give Him praise and glory for: WHO He is!!, and for WHAT he is able to do!

A grateful heart brings a smile to God. May we each make it our 'goal' to make God 'smile' every day! To verbally tell Him how much we love Him! One time I told the Lord I loved him more than chocolates! Then I made a commitment not to eat chocolate because of that love for Him until AFTER Christmas. It was my 'gift' to the Lord. After I had made my commitment it seemed like every place I went, people offered me, yes, chocolate! I would thank them and refuse. Some would say, I know you love it! Why not have just a bite! When I told them that I had made a promise to the Lord to not eat it until after Christmas, there was silence, and then an "Oh, okay!" Some would share with me things they had given up for Lent, and some would tell me it was good for me to do it.

When Christmas finally arrived, one of my friends who knew NOTHING about my promise gave me a present. Guess what that present was! It was 'brown and white candles' shaped like 'chocolates', that actually smelled like chocolate. This made me smile and laugh out loud! The Lord had acknowledged my sacrifice by guiding my friend to give me 'chocolate candles'. The candles shouted to me from the Lord: "This was a sweet odor of sacrifice in My sight!" It brings great joy to KNOW the Lord has received and acknowledged a gift. This is one of His special 'priceless' promises to each of us.

Time

Soon shall close thy earthly mission
Swift shall pass thy pilgrim days
Hope shall change to glad fruition
FAITH to SIGHT
PRAYER to PRAISE
"Jesus, I My Cross have Taken"
Henry F. Lyte 1793-1847

When we devote our lives to God's service, it is the Lord who guides our thoughts. Thomas Manton said, "We destroy our soul when we judge the mysteries of faith by common human reason."

We must remember the words of Fanny Crosby's hymn "Victory Through Grace":

"Not to the strong is the battle

Not to the swift is the race

Yet to the TRUE and the FAITHFUL

Victory is promised through GRACE."

We are instructed to 'forget the things behind' and to reach forth to that which is beyond.

Lord, grant that we may find mercy in this DAY and on THAT day to come. (my paraphrase of 2 Timothy 1:18)

Help us Lord to be strong in the grace, that is in Christ Jesus, to live DEAD to this world and ALIVE to God. Let Christ be ALL, and in ALL.

Help us Lord to put on "bowels of mercies, kindness, humbleness of mind, meekness, longsuffering, forbearing one another, and forgiving one another, and help us to forgive 'even as Christ forgave'; help us to 'put on charity, which is the bond of perfectness' and let 'the peace of God rule in our heart' , help us to 'be one body' and to be 'THANKFUL'.

May the word of Christ dwell in us richly in all wisdom, teaching and admonishing one another in psalms and hymns and spiritual songs, singing with grace in our heart as to the Lord; and whatsoever we do in word or deed, let us do all in the name of the Lord Jesus giving thanks to God the Father by Him; whatsoever we do, help us to do it heartily as to the Lord, and not unto men, knowing that of the Lord we shall receive the reward of the inheritance for we serve the Lord Christ. Help us to remember that no one is out of God's sight and help us to give you LORD all PRAISE, GLORY and HONOR – for ever and ever! (my paraphrase of Colossians 3:11-25).

Chapter 22

Life is Forever

Jesus said unto her, I am the resurrection and the life; he that believeth in me, though he were dead, yet shall he live: And whosoever liveth and believeth in me shall never die.

John 11:25, 26

There is a time when 'time' shall be 'no more'. Faith in the work of Jesus Christ who came, was obedient until death, and whom God raised from the dead, has proven that 'death' could not hold Him. And 'whosoever' believeth in Him, has been promised a home forever with Him. He has gone to prepare a place for us. (John 14:1)

He left living proof through those who saw him alive, appearing and disappearing, and walking through walls. His last appearance was before 500 witnesses before He was taken up in a cloud from the Mount of Olives recorded in the book of Acts.

Forever is not comprehendible because it is 'outside' of 'time'. We have been promised a place where there is no longer any sorrow, or tears, or suffering, for 'old things' have passed away, and He has made all things new.

In THIS Place

Most of our current life involves 'being busy' and requires 'focus, attention, and effort" upon earthly 'things'. Our days involve working, cleaning, and going places, then sleeping and rising to do everything all over again. This earth demands attention for us to survive, and at the end of long days, we crash and want 'distraction' and 'entertainment'. We use both to help us 'relax' and 'disconnect' from the 'stress' created by the forced march of daily responsibilities that demand every ounce of physical strength that we have.

Just caring daily for our physical bodies with exercise, bathing, caring for our teeth, eyes, hands and feet is time consuming.

Yet the beauty of this current world is beyond our ability to comprehend or understand. The birds alone are of such variety and different colors and beauty that they each appear as their very own 'work of art'. The butterflies as well, are uniquely different with an endless variety of patterns and colors, sizes and shapes, all of which come from a 'worm' that seems to hibernate and then bursts out of its shell with wings that give it flight.

Those who have the privilege of being in nature, who are able to go for walks in the woods, or sit beside streams, or the ocean, create poems that declare the wonder of what they behold. A world where every 'snowflake' is completely different, where every fingerprint or eye scan is completely different, SHOUTS the existence of a CREATOR.

In this world, we have the opportunity to BELIEVE and to walk in FAITH. We have the chance to CHOOSE to honor Him with our time and talents. We can read and be amazed at the promises contained in the Bible. We can CHOOSE to pray and ask for His help and to pray for others.

In THAT Place

The place we are going to will not have the stress and labor of life on earth. With supernatural bodies, we will have endless energy, and will be able to be transported miraculously by the Holy Spirit, from place to place. The 'beam me up Scottie' will become our reality.

The key to understanding what 'forever' will be like is contained within the book of Revelation. There we will proclaim the glory that is due the Creator of the Universe: "Blessing and glory, wisdom and thanksgiving, honor, and power and might be unto our God forever and ever, Amen" (Revelation 12:7).

John was shown a pure river proceeding out of the throne of God and of the Lamb, In the midst of the street of it, and on either side of the river, was there a tree of life, which bare twelve manner of fruits, and yielded her fruit every month, and the leaves of the tree were for the healing of the nations. And there shall be no more curse but the throne of God and of the Lamb shall be in it, and his servants shall serve him. And they shall see his face, and his name shall be in their foreheads. And there shall be no night there, and they need no candle, neither light of the sun, for the Lord God giveth them light and they shall reign for ever and ever (Revelation 22: 2-5).

Understanding What is To Come

My sister Audrey's kitten Grady is very interested in what is beyond the door that is at the top of the spiral staircase. He will travel up the stairs and sit and look at the light that shines through the crack under that door just waiting for the 'door' to open. He KNOWS something else is behind that door!

One day when I opened the door, I heard Grady headed my way. He was running as fast as he could to get to the spiral staircase. Up the stairs he came, so fast that he missed a step and went flying backward down three the steps, but he quickly stopped himself, and then rather than going back down, he turned and headed right back up as fast as he could. Now, he was standing at my feet on the top level, determined to get past my feet to go through the open door behind me. I moved my feet to block him and encourage him to return to the lower level, but he was absolutely determined. I reach down and picked him up in my arms and then carried him through my home. I showed him each room, and let him look out each of the windows. I spoke to him all the way through the home, telling him all about this wonderful new home that he now was able to occupy because he was in my arms. Then as I brought him back down to his home, I realized my awareness of 'heaven' makes me want to run as well to the Lord, in anticipating of just getting a 'glimpse' of what is to come! Heaven is REAL, and someday that 'door' for us will open, and we will also be ushered into the Kingdom that will never end!

Jesus told John, "Behold, I come quickly and my reward is with me to give to every man according to his work shall be. I am the Alpha and the Omega, the beginning and the End, the first and the last" (Revelation 22:12).

Chapter 23

Eternity Never Ends

Be of good cheer; I have overcome the world.

(Jesus)

John 16:33

Everything started within 'eternity' then the earth, sun and moon and galaxies were created, then man and women with free will choice. Currently, we live with the chaos and confusion that are allowed on earth for the purifying of our eternal souls. There is coming a time on earth that will allow for the 'restitution of all things'; a time when Jesus Christ returns to rule and reign with peace on earth for 1,000 years where the wolf will lie down with the lamb. And at the end of that 1,000 years, there will be a 'new heaven and a new earth' and we will be back to Eternity! Between now and then we are being refined by life's experiences. The very things that make us feel like we are 'dying' are making us into something more 'pleasing in the Lord's sight'. Like the pressed wild flowers (on the cover of this book) each very carefully placed inside the basket arrangement. Each pedal represents one of our trials on earth that we have successfully overcome. These are, even now, a 'sweet smelling savour unto the Lord'. These very things that we 'despise', the things that we 'do not desire' will be for us the very things that we will use to praise and give glory and honor to our God who lives and reigns forever.

What we have here on earth is the opportunity to glorify the Lord forever in eternity.

These are **God's Priceless, Precious Promises** - right here and now!
"I am the living bread which came down from heaven: if any man eat of this bread, he shall live forever: and the bread that I will give is my flesh, which I will give for the life of the world" (John 6:51).

Priceless -because these promises are **'sealed'**.
O Labour not for the meat which perisheth, but for that meat which endureth until everlasting life, which the son of man shall give unto you: for him hath God the Father SEALED" (John 6:27).

Precious- because these promises are **'eternal'**.
"Precious in the sight of the Lord is the death of His saints" (Psalm 116:15).
"And I give them eternal life, and they shall never perish, neither shall any man pluck them out of my hand. My Father, which gave them to me, is greater than all, and no man is able to pluck them out of my Father's hand" (John 10:28).

Start today to grab a hold of God's PROMISES!
Search for those promises like you would for a hidden treasure.
"Then shalt thou understand the fear of the Lord and find the knowledge of God" (Proverbs 2:5).

"O to be Like Thee"
Full of compassion
Loving, Forgiving
Lowly in Spirit
Holy and Harmless
Helping the Helpless
Cheering the fainting
Patient and Brave
Enduring cruel reproaching
Seeking the Wandering
Willing to Suffer
O to be Like **THEE**
Blessed Redeemer
Pure as Thy art
Come in Thy sweetness
Come in Thy fullness
Stamp Thine own image
Deep on my Heart!"   Thomas O. Chisholm 1866-1960

"Quicken thou me according to thy Word . . .
Quicken thou me in Thy way . . .
Quicken thou me in Thy righteousness" (Psalm 119: 35-40).

"Til heaven and earth pass not one jot or one tittle shall in no wise pass from the law until all be fulfilled" (Matthew 5:18).

"All flesh is grass, and all the goodliness thereof is as the flower of the field: the grass withereth, the flower fadeth: because the spirit of the Lord bloweth upon it: surely the people is grass. The grass withereth, the flower fadeth, but the word of our God shall stand forever."
(Isaiah 40: 6-8)

"May the objects of my life's pursuits be worthy of an immortal Spirit worthy of an heir of Heaven. Deliver me from whims and hobbies and nerve me for the infinite possibilities which are opening up before me."
Charles H. Spurgeon – "Flowers"

"Grace and peace be multiplied unto you through the knowledge of God, and of Jesus our Lord, according as his divine power hath given unto us all things that pertain unto life and godliness, through the knowledge of Him that hath called us to glory and virtue; whereby are **given unto us exceeding great and precious promises**: that by these ye may be partakers of the divine nature. . . add to your faith, virtue, and to virtue, knowledge, and to knowledge, temperance, and to temperance, patience, and to patience, godliness; and to godliness, brotherly kindness, and to brotherly kindness, charity."
 (2 Peter 1:2-7)

Lord, give us the spiritual rest of Your precious Holy Spirit and empower us with Your divine energy that we need for the activity within each moment of our day. May we understand that obedience and praise reflect your glory, just like a silver Hippo!

Bible Promises of the Return of Jesus Christ to Earth:

This same Jesus, which is taken up from you into heaven, shall so come in like manner as ye have seen him go into heaven. Acts 1:11

For the Lord himself shall descend from heaven with a shout, with the voice of the archangel, and with the trump of God: and the dead in Christ shall rise first: Then we which are alive and remain shall be caught up together with them in the clouds, to meet the Lord in the air: and so shall we ever be with the lord. 1 Thes. 4:16-17

The Disciples ask:

Tell us, when shall these things be? And what shall be the sign of thy coming, and of the end of the world?

And Jesus answered and said unto them, Take heed that no man deceive you. For many shall come in my name, saying, I am Christ; and shall deceive many.

And ye shall hear of wars and rumors of wars: see that ye be not troubled: for all these things must come to pass, but the end is not yet.

For nation shall rise against nation, and kingdom against kingdom, and there shall be famines, and pestilences, and earthquakes, in divers' places. All these are the beginning of sorrows. Then shall they deliver you up to be afflicted, and shall kill you: and ye shall be hated of all nations for my name's sake.

And then shall many be offended, and shall betray one another, and shall hate one another. And many false prophets shall rise, and shall deceive many. And because iniquity shall abound, the love of many shall wax cold. Matthew 24: 3-12

And this gospel of the kingdom shall be preached in all the world for a witness unto all nations; and then shall the end come. Matthew 24:14

For then shall be great tribulation, such as was not since the beginning of the world to this time, no, nor ever shall be. And <u>except those days should be shortened</u>, there should no flesh be saved; but for the elect's sake <u>those days shall be shortened</u>. Then if any man shall say unto you. Lo, here is Christ, or there; believe it not. For there shall arise false Christs, and false prophets, and shall shew great signs and wonders; insomuch that, if it were possible, they shall deceive the very elect. Behold, I have told you before. Wherefore if they shall say unto you, Behold, he is in the desert; go not forth: behold he is in the secret chambers; believe it not.

For as the lightning cometh out of the east, and shineth even unto the west; so, shall also the coming of the Son of man be. Matthew 24:21-27

But of that day and hour knoweth no man, no, not the angels of heaven, but my Father only.

But as the days of Noe were, so shall also the coming of the Son of man be. For as in the days that were before the flood they were eating and drinking, marrying and giving in marriage, until the day that Noe entered into the ark, and knew not until the flood came, and took them all away; so, shall also the coming of the son of man be. Matthew 24: 36-39

Watch therefore: for ye know not what hour your Lord doth come. Therefore, be ye also ready; for in such an hour as ye think not the son of man cometh. Matthew 24:42, 44

Denying ungodliness and worldly lusts, we should live soberly, righteously, and godly, in this present world; Looking for the blessed hope, and the glorious appearing of the great God and our Savior Jesus Christ. Timothy 2:12-13

Are you ready to meet Christ should He come today? You can be, if you are willing to accept Jesus Christ as your personal Savior.

The Provision of God: Salvation in Christ

But God commendeth his love toward us, in that, while we were yet sinners, Christ died for us. Romans 5:8

Who his own self bare our sins in his own body on the tree, that we, being dead to sins, should live unto righteousness: by whose stripes ye were healed. 1 Peter 2:24

He that believeth on the Son hath everlasting life; and he that believeth not the Son shall not see life; but the wrath of God abideth on him. John 3:36

Jesus saith unto him, I am the Way, the Truth, and the Life: no man cometh unto the Father, but by Me. John 14:6

Nether is there salvation in any other, for there is no other name unto heaven given among men, whereby we must be saved. Acts 4:12

. and the blood of Jesus Christ His Son cleanseth us from all sin. 1 John 1:7

The Prayer of Confession

That if thou shalt confess with thy mouth to the Lord Jesus, and shalt believe in thine heart that God hath raised Him from the dead, thou shalt be saved. For with the heart man believeth unto righteousness, and with the mouth confession is made unto salvation. Romans 10:9-10

Whosoever therefore shall confess me before men, him will I confess also before my Father which is in heaven. Matthew 10:32

MY PRAYER

"Lord Jesus, I am sorry for my sins, and I ask You to forgive me. I open the door of my heart, and receive You as my Lord and Savior. Take control of my life, and begin making me the person You want me to be. Thank you, Lord Jesus, for saving me and for hearing my prayer in Jesus' name. Amen"

The Power Available for the Christian Life

But ye shall receive power, after that the Holy Ghost is come upon you and ye shall be witnesses unto Me, both in Jerusalem, and in all Judea, and in Samaria, and unto the uttermost part of the earth. Acts 1:8

This I say then, walk in the Spirit, and ye shall not fulfil the lust of the flesh. Galatians 5:16

For God hath not given us the spirit of fear, but of power, and of love, and of a sound mind. 2 Timothy 1:7

But as it is written, eye hath not seen, nor ear heard, neither have entered into the heart of man, the things which God hath prepared for them that love Him. But God hath revealed them unto us by his Spirit; for the Spirit searcheth all things, yea, the deep things of God. 1 Corinthians 2:9-10

These things I have spoken unto you, that in Me ye might have peace. In the world ye shall have tribulation; but be of good cheer; I have overcome the world. John 16:33

King of Kings, Lord of Lords, Shepherd, and Bishop of our souls. 1Tmothy 6:15

The Royal High Priest, redeeming by His blood multitudes of every tribe, tongue, people, and nation. 1 Peter 2:9 Rev. 5:9

Head of the Church. Ephesians 1:22

Elect of God; power and authority are His. Matthew 28:18

Let Jesus be King of your life
Read your Bible every day to get to know Christ better.
Talk to God in prayer every day.
Find a church where the Bible is taught as the complete Word of God, and is the final authority.

RESOURCE:

Radio Bible Class (RBC) Ministries is a great resource for understandable and accessible information about Jesus Christ and His Holy Bible. They offer online guidance and a free monthly devotional entitled, *"Our Daily Bread"* that contains encouragement, comfort, and His divine guidance. To learn more on how to be ready for His return, visit: http://rbc.org/

If you enjoyed, "Experiencing God's Priceless, Precious Promises" I would love to hear from you:
Dawndensmore@gmail.com

**For more inspiring information
visit:**www.GodsAmazingWays.com

Other books written by Dawn Densmore-Parent:
DIVINE ENCOUNTERS: The Reality of God, Angels and Demons
Experiencing God's Amazing Ways
To order this book visit: Amazon.com or visit Kindle ebooks